*The only place where housework
comes before sewing is in the dictionary.*
MARY KURTZ

A to Z of Sewing

THE ULTIMATE GUIDE
for Beginning to Advanced Sewing

Martingale®
& COMPANY

A to Z of Sewing:
The Ultimate Guide for Beginning to Advanced Sewing
© 2008 Country Bumpkin Publications

First published in Australia in 2008 by
Country Bumpkin Publications
315 Unley Road
Malvern, South Australia 5061
Australia
www.countrybumpkin.com.au

Editor: Kathleen Barac

Assistant Editor: Anna Scott

Editorial Assistants: Ali Carpenter, Lizzie Kulinski,
Marian Carpenter, Heidi Reed

Illustrations: Kathleen Barac

Graphic Design: Lynton Grandison, Ann Jeffries,
Jenny James, Juliet Thomson

Photography: Andrew Dunbar Photography

Production Manager: Helen Davies

Publisher: Margie Bauer

First published in the United States in 2009 by
Martingale & Company
20205 144th Avenue NE
Woodinville, Washington 98072-8478
www.martingale-pub.com

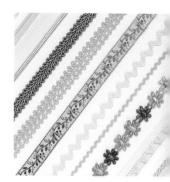

Printed in China
14 13 12 11 10   8 7 6 5 4 3 2 1

**Library of Congress Cataloging-in-Publication Data
is available upon request.**

ISBN: 978-1-60468-021-8

Mission Statement
*Dedicated to providing quality products
and service to inspire creativity.*

contents

Sew *(dictionary quote)*
TO JOIN OR TO DECORATE PIECES OF FABRIC BY MEANS OF A
THREAD REPEATEDLY PASSING THROUGH WITH A NEEDLE OR
SIMILAR IMPLEMENT

equipment

the sewing machine

The mechanics of sewing machines are constantly changing with new technology, but the main principles have remained the same. The fabric is moved under the presser foot by the feed dogs which are situated below the sole plate as the needle passes through the fabric. The correct amount of pressure ensures even feed and will depend on the weight of the fabric being used. Lightweight fabrics require light pressure and heavier fabrics require more pressure. A walking presser foot is usually available to help with difficult feed problems, such as when stitching suede or vinyl, or when quilting. Some tasks such as attaching buttons and free-motion embroidery do not require the feeding mechanism. Lowering the feed dogs below the stitch plate eliminates the movement.

A sewing machine is a vital piece of equipment for constructing a garment. Choose a machine that best suits your needs. Beginners will require very basic machine features such as straight and zigzag stitches, a well-formed buttonhole, some stretch stitches, and a small range of embroidery stitches. Familiarize yourself with your machine by studying the instruction manual and attending any workshops offered by the dealer.

Maintenance

Once you have a machine, taking good care of it ensures that it will last a long time. Lint and dust will collect under the sole plate and should be removed regularly to keep the machine working smoothly. This is particularly important if sewing velvet, corduroy, fleece, or other pile fabrics that may shed large amounts of lint.

Regular oiling will keep the machine working smoothly. Read the manual to determine if, where, and how often the machine should be oiled. Have it serviced annually by a qualified mechanic and keep it covered and in a dry place when not in use.

If traveling with your machine, place a soft fabric on the sole plate and lower the presser foot. Computerized machines can be temperamental and may not like being moved at all so be careful not to jostle it too much.

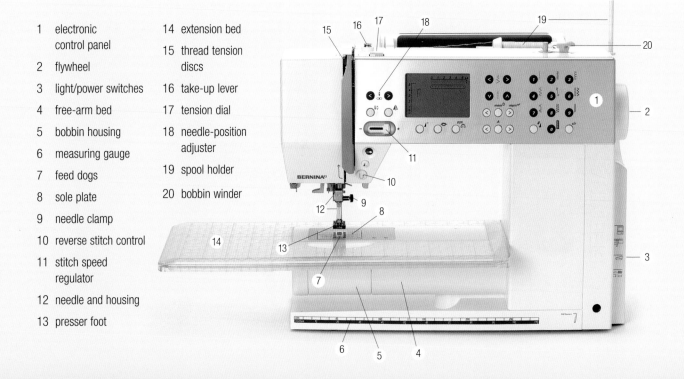

1   electronic control panel
2   flywheel
3   light/power switches
4   free-arm bed
5   bobbin housing
6   measuring gauge
7   feed dogs
8   sole plate
9   needle clamp
10 reverse stitch control
11 stitch speed regulator
12 needle and housing
13 presser foot
14 extension bed
15 thread tension discs
16 take-up lever
17 tension dial
18 needle-position adjuster
19 spool holder
20 bobbin winder

Stitching

Straight stitch is the most-used function of a sewing machine. To stitch a seam, the stitch length is usually set between 1.5 mm–2.5 mm, depending on the fabric being used. The thicker the fabric, the longer the stitch. Most machines also have a reverse action for back-stitching which is used to secure the line of stitching.

Zigzag stitching is generally used for finishing seams so that they don't ravel for appliqué and for heirloom sewing. The distance between the diagonal stitches is determined by the stitch length. Stitch width determines how far the needle moves from side to side—the higher the number, the wider the stitch.

Embroidery stitches are preprogrammed stitch patterns. Modern machines can work an infinite variety of embroidery motifs using built-in digital programs.

Stretch stitches are very strong and suitable for knit fabrics and elastic. They are produced by the needle moving forward or from side to side while the feed dogs are moving forward and backward. Some stretch stitches are perfect for sewing and finishing a seam at the same time.

Presser feet

Most machines come with a few standard, interchangeable presser feet. An all-purpose sewing foot, a zipper foot, an embroidery foot, and a buttonhole foot are the most basic. You can invest in others designed for specific purposes. Having the right foot on the machine makes it easier to achieve the best result for the task.

All-purpose sewing foot

This is the standard foot for all basic, forward-feed sewing. The sole of this foot is flat, providing control as the fabric passes over the feed dogs.

Blind-hem foot and edgestitch foot

These feet have a bar running through the center of the feet in front of the needle. Use the bar as a guide for instances when a line of stitching is required close to a ridge or fold, such as for hemming, edgestitching, or joining two pieces of lace with the edges butted together.

Buttonhole foot

Two grooves under the sole of a buttonhole foot allow the fabric to move freely as the thread builds up to form the end bars of the buttonhole. The guide between the grooves helps keep the side bars parallel and slightly apart.

Cording, piping, or beading foot

A large groove in the sole of these feet allows heavier threads, cording, and other high-relief decorative trims to pass freely under the foot after being stitched, as shown on page 143.

Darning foot

A darning foot is spring loaded, hopping over the surface while you move the fabric from side to side or backward and forward. This foot requires the feed dogs to be covered with a special stitch plate or to be lowered under the normal sole plate.

Embroidery foot

This foot is completely open in front of the needle, making the work clearly visible. There is also a wedge-shaped indentation under the foot, which allows dense satin (zigzag) stitching to glide through without becoming jammed. The angle in the indentation makes it possible to follow curves easily.

Pintuck foot

This is used with a twin needle to stitch pintucks, spacing the tucks by positioning the previous tuck in one of the grooves under the foot, as shown on page 142.

| Zipper feet | Buttonhole feet | Embroidery feet | Blind-hem feet | Rolled-hem feet | Darning foot |

Rolled-hem foot

The raw edge of the fabric is guided through a tunnel in this foot in front of the needle; it produces a perfectly folded and stitched narrow hem.

Zipper foot

This is a narrow, one-toed foot with notches on both sides for the needle positions. Adjust the foot or the needle position to stitch with the required side against the teeth of the zipper. A broad foot with rollers that uncurl the zipper coils is available for inserting invisible zippers.

Accessories

A walking foot works in unison with the lower feed dogs, passing the upper layers of fabric under the foot at the same rate.

The ruffler attachment allows long strips of fabric to be gathered quickly. It is good for soft furnishing projects.

A **spacer bar** and a **blind hem guide** are attachments for presser feet that enable the correct positioning of a line of stitching. A seam or hem gauge is fitted into a hole in the bed of the machine. The bar at the end of the guide is then positioned a specific distance from the needle.

the serger or overlocker

The main purpose of a serger is to finish the raw edges of a seam. Trimming is unnecessary because the serger trims as it sews, using a blade on one side of the stitch plate. It is not intended to be a replacement for a sewing machine.

A serger is similar to a sewing machine in that it has a presser foot to control the fabric and a feed system to pass the fabric through. A serger has at least two top threads that pass through a needle and two loopers, one upper and one lower, to form interlocking stitches over the raw edge. All the threads are tensioned by passing through discs and thread guides. Each has its own distinct path, often color coded, through the machine.

On a four-thread serger, which is the most common, there are two needle positions. For a more secure seam with a double line of straight stitching, use threads in both needles. When finishing seams and raw edges, use one needle only—the choice of left or right will depend on the desired width of the seam.

Accessories

A rolled-hem presser foot is invaluable for stitching tiny hems and seams on lightweight fabrics such as chiffon and organdy. Sometimes a special stitch plate is required as well as the foot. It is easier to work a rolled hem on curved edges using a serger.

A blind hem foot and a **gathering foot** are often available.

An elastic attachment can be a valuable tool, providing a quick way to attach elastic or decorative trims to a raw edge. The elasticity can be controlled by turning a screw on the attachment.

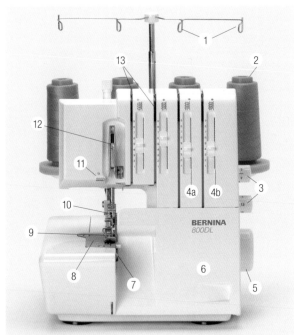

1	thread guides	7	cutting blade—behind cover
2	thread cones	8	stitch plate
3	stitch-length regulators	9	presser foot
4a	upper thread-looper tension discs	10	needle and housing
4b	lower thread-looper tension discs	11	thread guides
5	flywheel	12	take-up lever
6	lower looper housing	13	needle thread-tension discs

machine needles

Sewing-machine needles are available in different sizes, ranging from the finest (size 60) to the most coarse (size 110). Choose a needle that is suited to the type and weight of fabric that you are using and replace it regularly. Discard needles that are bent or burred because they are difficult to stitch with and they can damage the fabric. A damaged needle may also result in the machine skipping stitches.

Type	Description	Use	Size	Suitable for
Universal	Standard	General sewing	60, 70	Lightweight natural and synthetic fabric—chiffon, georgette, organdy, batiste
			70, 80	Synthetic silk, linen blends, lingerie fabrics, poplin, shirting
			80, 90	Ticking, linen, suiting
			90, 100	Coating
Jersey/Stretch	Ball point	Knit garments, swimwear	70	Fine jersey, single jersey
			75	Jersey, silk jersey
			80, 90	Lycra, lingerie fabrics
			90, 100	Knits (interlock, rugby)
Jeans	Extra sharp	Outer garments, sportswear	90–110	Canvas, corduroy, denim, heavy twill
Microtex	Extra sharp	Standard clothing	60–80	Microfiber, silk, cotton batiks
Embroidery	Large eye, highly polished, hollow neck, light ball point	Embroidery and specialty threads	75–90	Natural or synthetic fabrics
Hemstitch	Wing needle	Embroidery, hemstitching	100	Natural fabrics
Quilting	Light point	Straight and top stitching, decorative stitching	75–90	Natural or synthetic fabrics
Leather	Wedge-shaped point	Soft leather, vinyl	80, 90	Soft leather
			100	Leather and vinyl
Metafil	Standard point with large, long eye and deep groove	Metallic threads	80	Most natural or synthetic fabrics
Twin Needle	Standard needle, double shaft	Tucks, embroidery	70–100	Light- to mediumweight fabrics
Triple Needle	Standard needle, triple shaft	Tucks, embroidery	80	Light- to mediumweight fabrics

equipment

9

tools

Basic tools such as a good pair of scissors, selection of pins and needles, tape measure, and marking pens are essential to begin sewing. Adding more specialized equipment can be done over time.

Cutting tools

Dressmaking scissors, usually 7"–8" in length, make cutting out a garment easy. Use the full blade when cutting because this ensures a straight-cut edge. Buy the best quality you can afford and use them for cutting fabric only, since other materials will dull the blades.

Smaller sewing scissors, 4½"–5½" in length, are useful for trimming and clipping. Scissors are available with metal, plastic, or "soft grip" handles. Choose scissors that are comfortable to hold. Have scissors professionally sharpened as soon as they show signs of wear. Dead spots along the length or at the tip of the scissor blades are a common sign of wear. Keep them lubricated by occasionally placing a small drop of oil on the screw. Wipe away any excess before use.

Thread clippers are handy for small trimming tasks while you sew.

Rotary cutters are excellent for cutting bias binding or straight strips of fabric. They are used with a special self-healing mat underneath. Replace the blade as soon as it shows signs of wear.

A **seam ripper** makes unpicking stitches easy by cutting through the threads of a seam. It can also be used for cutting open buttonholes.

A **cutting table** provides a wonderful surface for laying and cutting out fabric. Most cutting tables are lightweight and can be folded up and stored when not in use.

Marking tools

Fabric marking pens are very handy for transferring any temporary pattern or design markings onto fabric. There are several different types available, so choose the one that best suits your needs.

Water-soluble markers are chemical based and make blue marks that can be removed with water. Do not iron before removing the marks because heat can make them permanent.

Disappearing ink (or air-soluble) markers are also chemical based and make a purple mark. Markings fade away quite quickly, depending on the fabric and the pressure used to mark. Do not iron before the marks fade.

Chalk pencils are used on dark fabrics. The chalk is enclosed in a wood casing, similar to a pencil. The marks brush away easily. Other forms of chalk markers are **seam markers** and **tailor's chalk.**

Dressmaker's carbon has a colored waxy surface on one side that is placed, facing the fabric, under the pattern. It is sold in a variety of colors—dark for light-colored fabrics and vice versa. Markings are transferred to the fabric with a scribing tool such as a tracing wheel. Mark only the wrong side of the fabric .

Measuring tools

The **tape measure** is any pliable measuring device. Choose a tape that has increments on both sides and is marked in imperial and metric measurements.

Long wooden or **metal rulers** are useful for marking long lines such as cutting lines, bindings, and bias strips.

A **sewing gauge** has a sliding tab, making it easy to measure pleats, the depth of a hem, the length of a buttonhole, and the spaces between them.

A **hem marker** is a useful tool to measure the level of a hem, making it consistent around a garment.

Pins and needles

There is a type of pin for every task. A good, all-purpose pin is a medium-length, glass-head pin with a fine shaft. Glass heads will not melt if ironed and are easy to find if dropped on the floor. Silk pins have a longer, finer shaft than regular pins and glide easily through fabrics. They are available with glass or plain heads. For hand sewing, crewel or Sharp needles in a selection of sizes are recommended.

Discard any pins or needles that are damaged in any way. Store your needles in their packets or a needle case. Pins should be kept in a moisture-proof container with a tight lid, to prevent rust. A small sachet of silica gel in the container will help.

General tools

Some tools and aids have been developed to make specific tasks easier.

A **point turner** makes pushing out tight corners easier.

A **loop turner** is a fine metal rod with a latch on the end which is used to turn belt loops and spagetti strap tubes right side out.

Bias-tape makers are used to fold the raw edges of binding strips continuously before they are pressed.

Pin cushions and **magnets** help to contain pins and needles in one place.

A **needle threader** is often helpful to thread machine and hand-sewing needles.

Thimbles are available in different materials such as plastic, leather, and metal. A thimble protects the top of the finger that is used to push the needle through the fabric. Choose a thimble that fits snugly over your finger.

Aids such as *anti-fray sprays* and liquids, *fusible tapes*, *glues*, and *basting sprays* are available. Before using these products on any fabric, read the manufacturer's instructions carefully.

fabric

The infinite variety of fabrics available can be reduced to three main elements—fiber content, weight, and the way it's contructed. There are two main types of fiber used to make fabric—natural and synthetic. Weaving, knitting, and bonding are the processes used to turn yarn into fabric. The weight of the fabric can range from a voile so sheer you can see through it to the heavy worsted woolen fabrics used for suits and coats.

fiber content

Natural fibers such as cotton, wool, silk, and linen have all the subtle irregularities and intrinsic beauty present in nature. They are absorbent and porous, making them very reactive to dyes, temperature, and humidity. Cotton and wool especially are comfortable to wear in very different climatic situations, and a garment made from silk enables the wearer to remain cool on hot days and warm in cold conditions.

Natural fibers may have a limited lifespan and they may be susceptible to insect damage or mildew. However, with appropriate care, they can be very long lasting.

Linen is one of the world's oldest fibers. It is manufactured from the fibrous stalks of the flax plant and comes in various weights for different purposes. Ramie refers to a fiber from the nettle family of plants, mainly grown in Asia. It is sometimes blended with cotton for less-expensive clothing and is often confused with linen. Its care is similar to linen, but if blended with other fibers, follow the manufacturer's care instructions.

Silk yarn is the longest natural filament used to make fabric. It is produced when the cocoon of the silkworm is unwound. Wild silk (tussah) is made from the cocoons of silkworms that live in uncultivated conditions and eat a varied diet. It is naturally dark in color and cannot be bleached.

Synthetic fibers are produced in a laboratory using chemical processes that combine elements such as petroleum products, alcohol, gasses, water, or air. This class of fabrics include polyester, nylon, acrylic, lycra, polyurethane, and metallic fibers such as Lurex. Rayon was the first synthetic fiber, developed as a more affordable replacement for silk.

Viscose and acetate are also synthetic fibers but they are made from cellulose—a natural plant-based product.

Synthetic fabrics are very strong and resilient but lack the absorbancy and temperature-transference properties of natural fibers.

Blended fibers are produced by combining natural and synthetic fibers to contain the best attributes of both. Polycotton, a blend of polyester and cotton, is the most widely used blend. It combines the strength and crease resistance of polyester with the comfort and softness of cotton.

woven, nonwoven, or knitted

Weaving is the interlacing of yarns on a machine called a loom. The stronger warp yarns are fixed lengthwise and interwoven at right angles with the often weaker weft yarn.

There are three main weaves—plain, twill, and satin. A plain weave is a thread being passed under and over the warp threads in one row, and then alternating the passing sequence in the next row.

In a twill weave, the weft thread passes over two or more warp threads in one row and moves one thread to the right or left in each successive row. This forms diagonal ridges on the surface of the fabric.

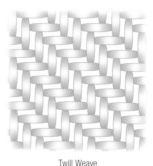

Twill Weave

Satin weave is more complex, with warp threads covering weft thread so no twill line is visible. Patterned weaves, such as dobby, damask, and jacquard, are complex structures that produce an intricate, textured surface with areas of satin-weave pattern against a plain or twill background.

Knit fabrics are based on the age-old technique of knitting by hand. Knitting machines produce fabrics with a similar structure with stitches on a much smaller scale. Complicated knit variations can be produced by changing the arrangement of knit and purl stitches. Rows of loops formed along the length of a knit fabric are called ribs. Another feature of knit fabrics is elasticity. This makes them particularly suited to use for casual clothing and sportswear.

Nonwoven fabrics are produced with processes such as felting and netting.

Felting is the oldest method of making fabric. Short fibers are matted together using heat, moisture, and agitation or pressure, creating a thick, pliable sheet that doesn't fray.

Netting is a twisted or knotted structure that produces an open mesh. Tulle and cotton net are plain styles of netting. To make lace, intricate floral or geometric patterns are woven into the mesh, using finer or coarser threads than those forming the netting.

interfacing

When constructing a garment, interfacing can be applied to the wrong side of the fabric pieces to provide shape and stability. Interfacings come in light-, medium-, and heavyweight and can be stitched or fused to the fabric. They may be woven or nonwoven and consist of natural or synthetic fibers. The colors are limited to white, black, gray, and ecru. Choose an interfacing that matches the care requirements and weight of your fabric, remembering that the interfacing should always be the same weight or lighter than the garment fabric and that your pattern may require more than one type. For sheer fabrics where interfacing may show through, using another layer of the garment fabric is a good alternative to interfacing.

Precut interfacings for waistbands, cuffs, and button bands have seam-line and fold markings that make it easier to keep the seams and folds evenly spaced.

Woven interfacings are usually cut on the straight grain, matching the grain of the fabric piece. Nonwoven interfacing has no grain and can be cut in any direction.

Stretch or knit interfacings have a certain amount of crosswise stretch, making them ideal for knit fabrics.

Interfacings are generally attached to facings or linings, but lightweight types often work better when applied to the garment pieces. Personal preference can play a large part in determining on which layer the interfacing is placed, bearing in mind that it should never be obvious on the right side of the garment.

care symbols

Common symbols appearing on garment or fabric labels provide care instructions from the manufacturer.

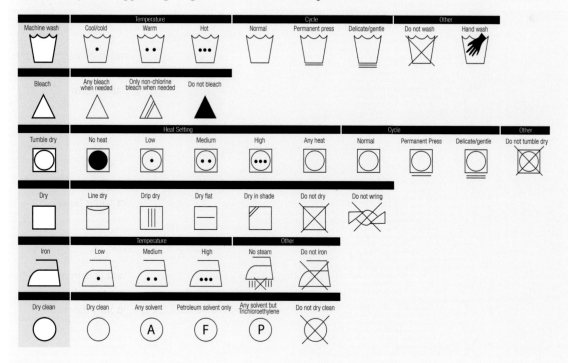

fabric content

Care instructions are intended as a guide only. It is advisable to check the manufacturer's instructions before you launder because individual fabrics may have more specific requirements.

Type	Fabric	Features	Care instructions
Cotton	Batiste, broadcloth, *broderie anglaise,* buckram, calico, chambray, chintz, corduroy, damask, denim, duck, flannelette, gingham, homespun, lace, lawn, muslin, net, organdy, piqué, poplin, sailcloth, sateen, seersucker, terry cloth, ticking, velvet, velveteen, voile, waffle	Cool to wear. Absorbant, porous, and accepts dyes easily. Strong fiber but tends to crease easily. Deteriorates with mildew and color fades in sunlight. Shrinks unless treated, so preshrink before use.	Warm to hot machine wash. Can be bleached and tumble dried. Iron while damp.
Wool	Broadcloth, challis, crepé, flannel, gabardine, serge, tweed, worsted	Insulating properties make it warm to wear. Flame and wrinkle resistant. Susceptible to moth damage.	Dry clean. Shrink-resistant wools may be machine washed. Steam iron. Use pressing cloth.
Silk	Batiste, broadcloth, brocade, charmeuse, chiffon, crepe de chine, georgette, habutai, lace, organza, shantung, tussah silk, velvet	Soft, lustrous fabric that drapes well. Cool or warm to wear. Deteriorates with mildew and perspiration. Fades in sunlight. Susceptible to moth damage.	Usually dry clean; some may be washed if softness is required. Cool iron on the wrong side.
Linen	Damask, handerchief linen, suiting, many medium- to heavyweight fabrics with a textured surface	Strong, absorbent fiber. Draws heat from the body, making it cool to wear. Creases easily and has a tendency to shrink.	Dry clean to keep crisp, polished finish.
Synthetic	Acetate, acrylic, lace, lycra, nylon, rayon, satin, taffeta, tulle	Crease resistant. Some have a silk-like luster, drape well, and dry quickly. Most collect static electricity. Acrylics have low absorbancy and resist wrinkles, moths, and mildew. Have a tendency to pill.	Launder fabrics according to their specific requirements.
Blends	Batiste, broadcloth, brocade, *broderie anglaise,* chambray, chiffon, chintz, damask, gabardine, gingham, homespun, lawn, muslin, piqué, polycotton, seersucker, voile	Being a blend of two or more fibers, the combination is designed to highlight the best properties of each.	Launder according to the most sensitive fiber in the blend.
Knits (silk, cotton, wool, blended fibers)	Bouclé, double knit, fleece and polar knits, jersey, rib, rugby, stretch terry, tricot, velour	Strong fibers and construction. High polyester content ensures crease resistance and durability but may have a tendency to pill.	Follow care instructions for the fiber used.
Nonwoven	Felt, fur, leather, plastic, suede, vinyl	Materials used for their durability and strength. These features can make them difficult to stitch.	Plastic and vinyl can be wiped clean—all others should be dry cleaned.

notions

Notions are the additional items besides the fabric and pattern that you'll need to finish your garment.

buckles and clasps

Belts, shoulder straps, and swimwear pieces are some instances where these types of fastenings are used.

Buckles can be bought as a complete unit or as bare metal or plastic to be covered with fabric.

An **overall buckle** comes in two pieces—the clip, which is secured onto the end of the straps through adjuster bars, and a metal jean button that is attached to the bib with a rivet.

A **swimsuit bra hook** is used to secure the narrow ends of a bra top at the midriff.

elastic

Most elastics are made from a rubber core covered in cotton or synthetic thread. Elastic is available as a single strand, such as shirring and hat elastic, or as several rows braided together. When choosing elastic, look for one with the most suitable features for the style and use of the garment.

Braided elastics can be identified by the lengthwise parallel ridges that give them a stronger grip. This type of elastic narrows when stretched and is recommended for use in casings rather than stitching to the garment itself.

Woven elastics are usually softer and the edges curl less when stretched than the braided types. This makes them more suitable to stitch directly onto the fabric.

Non-roll elastic is constructed with vertical ribs to keep it from twisting within a casing or on a waistband.

lace

Lace is available in dress-width yardage or in quite narrow widths used as trimming. Styles range from delicate mesh laces like malines or Valenciennes to more sturdy types such as cluny and guipure. *Broderie anglaise,* an embroidered eyelet lace, is another widely used trimming.

Lace can also be divided into groups according to the number of decorative or straight edges it has. Edging lace has one decorative edge and one straight edge, which is used to attach it to the fabric.

Insertion lace has two finished edges, often decorative. This is either applied to the right side of the fabric so that the fabric shows through, or is inserted between two pieces of fabric. Beading lace (which can be either edging or insertion lace) has a series of decorative holes along the center or to one edge for ribbon to be threaded through.

ribbon, braid, and cord

Ribbons are used to decorate garments and home decor items. Some forms are satin, velvet, moiré, looped or ruffle edge, grosgrain, petersham, and woven jacquard ribbon with delicate woven designs. They may be stitched flat, threaded through beading lace, folded into bows, used as ties and sashes, or rolled and folded into three-dimensional roses and rosebuds—the uses are endless.

Braids are bulkier and have more texture than ribbons. Some of the most common types are silky, soutache, and scroll braids. Soutache is stitched to the fabric along the center groove. The others are stitched along both edges.

Rickrack has zigzag edges and is often classed as a braid. It can be stitched flat, shaped to follow a curve, or stitched into a seam to expose the points along one edge.

Twisted cords made from cotton or rayon are used in drawstring casings or home furnishings. Fine cotton cording is enclosed in fabric to make corded piping or used plain to define twin-needle pintucks.

tapes and binding

Cotton tapes stabilize seams that would otherwise stretch, adding structure and firmness. Fusible tapes eliminate the need to tack or secure with stitching.

Belt backing or waistband stiffening is fused to one side of a waistband or slipped through a fabric belt to provide stability and support.

Seam binding is used to finish a raw edge. It is cut on the bias, allowing it to be shaped to fit a curve. Binding is available in several widths and dozens of colors. Satin bias binding makes an attractive alternative to plain fabric types.

Boning is made from nylon or plastic and is used to add shape and support to the seams of a bodice, usually in strapless styles. It is threaded through a channel sewn into the seam allowance. Covered boning is simply stitched to the seam allowance along the sides of the tape covering.

beads, sequins and other trinkets

Embellishing your garments is easy with the many different forms of beads, sequins, jewels, and charms available. Designing your decoration and stitching the elements on individually may be time consuming. Ready-made motifs are quickly attached by sewing around the edge by hand or machine.

fasteners

Zippers are available in three main types—conventional, separating, and invisible. Conventional and invisible dress zippers are divided at one end while separating zippers come apart at both ends for use in jackets.

All zippers consist of metal or nylon teeth embedded into fabric tape or a synthetic coil stitched to fabric tape. A metal or plastic slider opens and closes the interlocking teeth of the zipper. Metal clips or melted nylon "stops" are positioned at the upper and lower ends to prevent the slider from slipping off.

Buttons are probably the oldest form of closure. Originally made from bone, they were stitched on with dried sinew and pushed through holes in an animal hide. Although styles have changed, the button is still one of the most common forms of garment closure.

Buttons are available in an infinite number of styles, sizes, shapes, and colors. When choosing ones that are right for the garment, keep in mind that a novelty button with sharp or odd angles may not be a suitable or practical form of closure. They are difficult to pass through a buttonhole and are best used as decoration only.

Fabric-covered buttons provide a suitable alternative when the perfect ready-made button cannot be found. When making your own, follow the manufacturer's instructions carefully to obtain professional results.

Hook-and-loop tape is also known as **Velcro**. The surface of one tape has a fuzzy, looped nap that locks into the hooked nap of the other tape when pressed together. It is available in various widths and colors.

threads

Sewing thread should be strong, durable, and pliable, ensuring it will resist breaking under the strain of passing through the machine under tension. It is important to match the needle size to the thread you are using. If the needle is too small, the thread will fray and break easily. If the needle size is too large, the thread will not fill the needle holes punctured through the fabric.

Thread sizes are expressed as a number—the higher the number, the finer the thread. A mediumweight thread suitable for most fabrics is size 50.

Natural sewing threads include cotton, silk, and linen. Cotton and silk are both suitable for machine sewing. Linen and strong cotton threads, wrapped around a

polyester core, are usually confined to hand-sewing tasks that require extra thread strength.

Synthetic threads are made from spun polyester or sometimes nylon. There are also polyester and cotton blends, which are strong all-purpose threads.

All threads have a silicone or polished finish which allows them to pass through the machine and the fabric with ease.

Choose a thread slightly darker than the background color for plain fabrics. For prints, checks, or plaids, the thread color should match the dominant fabric color.

General-purpose threads have a spun polyester core wrapped in cotton. They are stronger and have more elasticity than other threads and are suitable for all fabrics. This thread comes in the widest range of colors and weights.

Pure cotton threads are used for a wide variety of tasks, from fine heirloom sewing to quilting and topstitching by hand or machine. They are usually finished with a process called mercerizing, which gives a lustrous sheen. Cotton threads do not have much give and are therefore not recommended for use with knit fabrics.

Silk is a fine, strong sewing thread with a soft, pearly sheen. It is used for silk lingerie, heirloom baby gowns, and some fine woolen fabrics.

Metallic thread usually has a cotton or polyester core, loosely wrapped with a gold, silver, or copper metallic fiber. It is commonly used for hand or machine embroidery. Treat it carefully when pressing because these threads do not respond well to heat or steam.

Invisible thread made from nylon or polyester is a strong, transparent monofilament that comes in two shades—light and dark. It is commonly used for hems and can be useful when you are unable to find a thread shade to match your fabric.

measurements

Accurate body measurements are essential for choosing the appropriate pattern size and for making any adjustments to obtain the best fit. Have a friend help you with these. Take the measurements in bare feet, wearing only undergarments or figure-hugging clothing. Tie a ribbon around your waist and adjust it to your natural waistline.

Height. Stand straight with your back against a wall. Place a ruler on top of your head and at 90º to the wall. Mark the wall at the end of the ruler. Step away and measure your height from the floor to the mark.

Bust. (On children or men, this is the chest measurement). Place the tape measure around your chest with the tape across the fullest part of the bust and the widest section of the back.

Bust point. Take a measurement between the high point of the shoulder and the tip of the breast.

Waist. Measure around the waist at the position of the ribbon. Leave the ribbon in place as a marker for other measurements.

Hips. Measure around the fullest part of the hips and bottom.

Back length. Measure from the base of the neck to the waist marker at the back.

Shoulder. Place the tape measure from the natural neckline to the edge of the shoulder joint.

Sleeve length. With your hand on your hip, measure from the shoulder joint over the elbow and down to the wrist.

Trouser length. Measure along the side of one leg from the waist marker to the ankle joint, or the preferred trouser length.

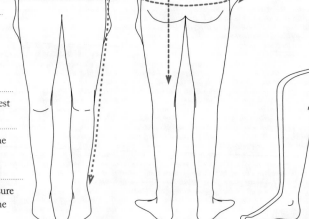

Skirt length. Measure from the waist marker at the back, over the fullness of the bottom, and down to the preferred length for the style of skirt.

Neck. Place the tape measure around your neck at the lowest position where it joins the shoulder line.

Crotch length. Measure the distance from the waist at the front, between the legs, and up to the waist at the back. Roughly divide this measurement in two at a midpoint between the legs and record it as the front and back crotch lengths.

Crotch depth. Sitting on a solid flat chair, straighten your back and measure between the waist marker and the seat of the chair at your side.

patterns

A pattern is a set of templates provided so that a copy can be made of an original model. A sewing pattern contains not only the pattern pieces but also additional information.

pattern cover

Photographs or drawings on the pattern envelope show the style and form of the original garment or object. The front and back view drawings will give an indication of the complexity of the project. Besides the main garment design, patterns usually have alternative styling options.

On the back, charts display standard body measurements in metric and imperial units, as well as finished garment measurements and the fabric, lining, interfacing, and notions required for each size. There are also suggestions for suitable fabrics to use.

size

Patterns are drafted from a set of standard body measurements based on the average sizes of the population. Refer to page 18 for taking measurements. Your pattern size may be the same as your ready-to-wear size, however a sewing-pattern size should be directly related to your measurements. The actual measurements of a pattern will not exactly match yours. Except for garments made from stretch fabrics, a garment should have room for the wearer to stretch, bend, reach, and walk. This is called "wearing ease" and is already incorporated into the pattern. Patterns designed specifically for knit fabrics include less wearing ease because the fabric stretches. Woven fabrics should not be substituted in patterns for stretch knits because there will not be enough wearing ease to make the garment comfortable.

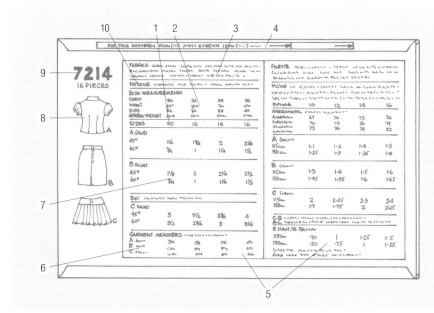

The pattern envelope back

1. sizes included
2. standard body measurements
3. suggested fabrics
4. stretch indicator if applicable
5. pattern statistics, measurements, and conversions
6. finished garment measurements
7. fabric requirements for each view
8. back view illustrations
9. pattern catalogue number
10. notions required

Specific body measurements will determine the pattern size for different garment types. As the fit is closer on the upper body, the size of a woman's dress, coat, shirt, or jacket pattern is chosen by the bust measurement. For men and children, use the chest measurement as the primary measurement. Trousers and skirt sizes are chosen by the hip measurement, which should be the main consideration when a pattern contains both upper and lower garments. If any measurement falls between the standard measurements, choose the larger size.

Multi-sized patterns

These patterns have cutting lines for several sizes printed on the same pattern piece. Each size has a unique line style—with a different arrangement of dashes or dots. A solid line usually denotes a line common to all sizes.

Trace the lines and markings for the desired size onto lightweight interfacing or tracing paper. Tracing the pieces keeps the original pattern intact and tracings are more durable than tissue paper. You can also make slight adjustments between the lines to take your own measurements into account. For instance, your waistline might be the same as one of the smaller sizes but your hips match a larger one. Draw a line between the two on your tracing.

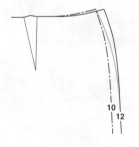

symbols

Pattern pieces are defined by a series of lines, arrows, dots, and symbols common to all pattern brands. The pattern symbols are usually explained in a chart. Solid or dashed outer lines, marked with a size, are the cutting lines. Seam allowances are marked with a particular measurement or a line of long dashes.

Every pattern piece should have a straight line with arrows at both ends, denoting the direction of the fabric grain. It is important to pin the pattern piece to the fabric aligning the grain line.

Pairs of solid adjustment lines are printed at the best positions to make alterations to the length of a pattern piece. If there is more than one set of double lines, it is best to divide the adjustment between the positions rather than make it all in one place.

Triangular notches indicate points to align when matching the raw edges of two garment pieces. Bent arrows show that an edge should be placed on the fold when cutting. Other markings may include zipper, buttonhole, button, pleat, dart, and interfacing placement symbols. Most symbols should be transferred to the wrong side of the fabric after cutting.

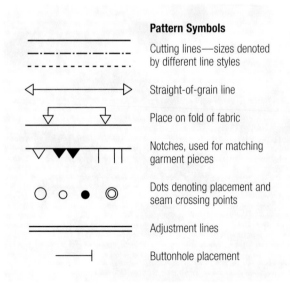

Pattern Symbols

Cutting lines—sizes denoted by different line styles

Straight-of-grain line

Place on fold of fabric

Notches, used for matching garment pieces

Dots denoting placement and seam crossing points

Adjustment lines

Buttonhole placement

altering patterns

When making adjustments to any pattern piece, always stitch a mock-up (or muslin) using an inexpensive fabric first. Further alterations may be necessary before cutting into your final fabric. Any changes should be made to all corresponding pattern pieces.

Lengthening

Cut through the pattern piece between the adjustment lines. Center a piece of tracing paper under the separation point. Spread the two pattern pieces for the required distance. Keep the "place on fold" line matching if the piece has one, otherwise center the lower piece under the upper piece. Check the distance with a ruler and tape or pin the pattern pieces to the paper. Continue any pattern lines on the paper (Fig. 1). Trim away any excess paper.

For a skirt, tape or pin a piece of paper at the lower edge of the pattern piece. Using a ruler, measure and mark dots for the new hemline at approximately 2" intervals below the curve. Join the dots and then mark a line to extend the sides (Fig. 2).

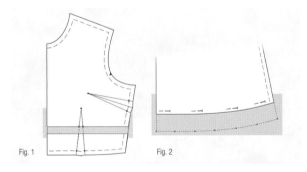

Fig. 1

Fig. 2

Shortening

Measure and mark a line below the uppermost adjustment line at the required distance. Fold the pattern piece on the adjustment line and bring the fold down to meet the new line. Tape or pin in place, ensuring any "place on fold" lines are straight. If the sides are uneven, redraw the lines to meet on the upper and lower edges of the pleat formed in the pattern piece (Fig. 3).

For a skirt, measure and mark dots for the new hemline at approximately 2" intervals above the curve. Join the dots and trim off the excess (Fig. 4).

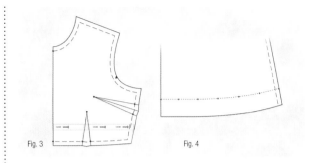

Fig. 3

Fig. 4

Adjusting the shoulder width

To prepare a pattern piece for a shoulder alteration, mark a line from the center of the shoulder, roughly parallel to the armhole. Mark another line to the armhole notch. Shoulder adjustments should be done on both the front and back bodice pieces.

Increasing the width of the shoulder. Cut through the marked lines. Keeping the armhole points touching, spread the armhole and shoulder corner until the shoulder line matches your measurement. Tape a piece of paper behind and secure. Redraw the shoulder line between the outer points (Fig. 5).

Decreasing the shoulder width. Cut through the marked lines. Rotate the shoulder corner inward, overlapping the pieces until the shoulder line matches your measurement. Tape together and redraw the shoulder line between the outer points (Fig. 6).

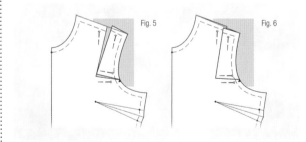

Fig. 5

Fig. 6

Adjusting the bust dart

A small adjustment to the height of a bust dart may be achieved by simply raising or lowering the bust point. For large adjustments, the entire dart should be raised or lowered to ensure the correct fit. Measure 1" from the point of the bust dart and compare your measurement to this point (Fig. 7, page 22).

Lowering the bust dart. Cut horizontally across the pattern above the dart and vertically down past the dart point. Pleat the pattern below the dart for the depth required to lower the bust point. Tape a piece of paper behind the pattern and secure. Redraw the side edge between the armhole and the dart. Lower the point of the waist dart by the same measurement (Fig. 8).

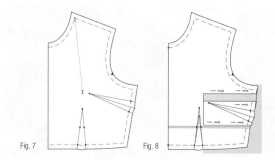

Fig. 7   Fig. 8

Raising the bust dart. Cut across the pattern below the dart and vertically up past the dart point. Pleat the pattern above the dart for the depth required to raise the bust point. Tape a piece of paper behind the pattern and secure. Redraw the side edge. Increase the point of the waist dart by the same measurement (Fig. 9).

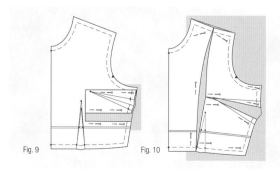

Fig. 9   Fig. 10

Increasing the bust fullness. Cut vertically from the inside edge of the waist dart to the center of the shoulder. Cut horizontally from the center front to the bust point and along the center of the dart. Place paper behind the pattern and spread the pieces apart. Keep the shoulder and lower edge points touching on the vertical line. Example: To increase the bust measurement from 38" to 42", spread the pieces sideways by 2" (half of the desired increase). Increase the length to match your bust-point measurement. Tape the pieces in place and redraw the dart (Fig. 10).

Adjusting the crotch

Changing the hip and waist measurements alone will not entirely allow for a large tummy or a flat bottom. The crotch length and depth should also be adjusted to ensure the correct fit.

Increasing the waist or hip. Make changes in small increments at the side seams (Fig. 11). Larger adjustments should be distributed between the side seams, darts, and the crotch seam on both the front and back pieces.

Fig. 11

Adjusting the length at the crotch point. The following alteration is the easiest way to lengthen the crotch, but it also changes the width at the top of the legs. Mark a new crotch point inside or outside the cutting line and redraw the line, tapering to join with the original line (Fig. 12).

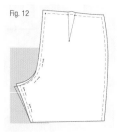

Fig. 12

Adjusting the depth. Spread out or pleat the pattern at the adjustment line for the required distance on both the front and back pieces (Fig. 13).

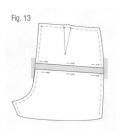

Fig. 13

Increasing the length at the crotch seam. Cut through the adjustment line. Spread the crotch seam only for the required distance. Tape a piece of paper behind and redraw the crotch line (Fig. 14).

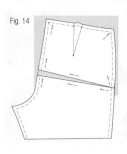

Fig. 14

Decreasing the length at the crotch seam. Pleat the adjustment line for the required distance at the crotch seam only, tapering the fold to the side seam. Redraw the crotch line to straighten (Fig. 15).

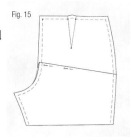

Fig. 15

preparing the fabric

Fabric preparation is essential before you start cutting. If the fabric has been folded on a bolt, check to see if the fold line can be pressed out when required and to ensure it is not faded.

Hold the fabric up to the light to see if there are any holes or flaws that should be avoided. If you find any, mark them and place them right side up when you lay the fabric out to ensure you avoid them when you pin the pattern pieces onto the fabric.

Preshrink fabrics containing fibers with a tendancy to shrink, referring to the fabric chart on page 14. To prepare the fabric, preshrink it by laundering following the manufacturer's care instructions.

grain

When choosing woven fabric you should be aware of how its characteristics may affect garment construction.

The grain of a fabric is indicated by the direction of the yarns; the warp is lengthwise and the weft, crosswise. Any diagonal dissection of the warp and the weft is the bias. The true bias is the 45˚ angle between them.

The way a garment hangs or drapes is affected by the grain on which it is cut. Lengthwise grain is the strongest and has very little give or stretch. In most garments this hangs vertically, taking the weight of the garment from shoulder to hem. Crosswise grain is more pliable and drapes differently, giving the garment a softer appearance. Bias grain has the most stretch, allowing it to drape softly. A bias-cut dress or skirt should be hung and left until the sections with the greatest stretch have dropped to their lowest level before the hem is marked and stitched in place.

The selvage is the firmly woven strip that forms along each lengthwise edge of the finished fabric. Very few pieces of fabric have both selvages and grainlines perfectly aligned and at right angles to each other. To achieve the correct alignment, cut the upper and lower edges following a thread in the fabric weave, either by sight or by pulling a thread and cutting along the channel that appears.

Straightening the grain

Fold the fabric in half along the length, matching the selvages and the upper, cut edge. Hold up the length and check if the selvages stay aligned, or if they fall away from each other.

If they remain aligned or there is very little difference over the entire length of the fabric, simply lay it out and cut out the garment pieces.

A greater difference in the way the selvages hang may be corrected by pressing. If the fabric is really skewed, you may need to review the suitability of the fabric.

Fabric may also be tugged sharply on the bias to bring the yarns back into alignment. Move from the upper corner with the most distortion to the opposite lower corner. This process is best done with two people.

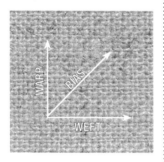

Printed stripes and checks with an obvious off-grain print will make the fabric look crooked even if the grainlines are aligned. Since it is part of the fabric, this cannot be corrected. Check the print in the store and avoid buying fabric with this type of flaw.

surface direction

Textured fabrics like velvet, velveteens, and corduroy have a napped surface or pile, which changes appearance when placed in the opposite direction. If the pile faces downward, the color appears lighter and the surface has a delicate sheen. In the opposite direction, the color is rich and dense with no sheen at all. Choose the direction you like the best and mark with an arrow on the selvages. Remember to place each pattern piece in this direction on the layout.

Fabric direction should also be consistent for fabrics with a "shot" weave and for some satins. Check satin fabric by placing two swatches side by side in opposite directions in daylight. If the color remains the same then it may be possible to rotate pattern pieces on the layout. The same applies for shot fabrics. Choose the color you like best and lay all the pieces in this direction. The play of light will change the colors with movement; laying out the pieces in the same direction will mean the changes will be consistent.

right and wrong side

The right side is often obvious, however at times you may need to study the fabric carefully to determine the right and wrong sides.

The right side of the fabric has generally been finished to resist marks and pilling. There is no rule to say you can't use the wrong side as the right if you prefer. When there is no apparent difference between the right and wrong sides, choose one and mark this side on all the pieces.

Smooth fabrics usually have a delicate sheen on the right side and appear dull on the wrong. Intricate weaves like jacquards and dobby cottons are smoother on the right side with loose loops of carried thread on the wrong side. Printed designs are sharper and brighter on the right side and less distinct on the wrong side.

pattern pieces

Identify all the pattern pieces needed for the chosen view of the garment you are making. Consider any style changes you may wish to make, such as eliminating, or repositioning pockets.

Cut the pattern pieces from the sheets or trace them onto interfacing or tracing paper to preserve the original. This is useful when making alterations, because the altered pattern will only fit the intended wearer. Return all the unused pieces to the envelope to avoid confusion later on. Carefully press out any creases from the pattern pieces with a lukewarm dry iron.

Alter the pattern if necessary, ensuring that the alterations are visible on both sides and that the same alterations have been done on all the corresponding pieces, such as facings. The length should be checked and altered if necessary before cutting out.

cutting layouts

The cutting layouts are an import feature of the pattern. They are usually found on the instruction sheet, along with a numbered list of the pattern pieces to identify them on the layouts. Find the layouts for the chosen view and the width of the fabric you are using.

Fabrics with a napped surface should be cut out following a "with nap" layout. If there is no layout for your fabric width or if you are changing any design details, you may need to do a trial layout based on the fabric width that's closest to the one you are using.

Work on the longest surface available. It should be long enough to accommodate the full length of the fabric if possible so that you don't disturb the layout until you have cut out all the pieces.

Determine how the fabric should be folded from the layout. To avoid a permanent mark along the center of the fabric, use double lengthwise folds. Selvages and design features such as stripes, checks, and printed or woven patterns should align exactly. For slippery or sheer fabrics that shift easily, pin the selvages together at short intervals.

When positioning the pattern piece, take note of the pattern placement direction if you have one marked.

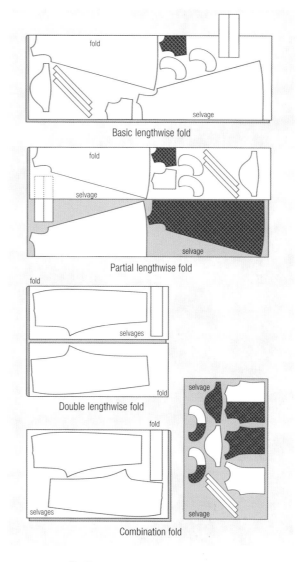

Basic lengthwise fold

Partial lengthwise fold

Double lengthwise fold

Combination fold

hints cutting layouts

Placing matching pieces in opposite directions should only occur on fabrics with no obvious nap or direction.

Shaded or partly shaded pattern pieces should be placed with the writing face down for that area.

Pieces extending or with dashed lines should be placed on a single layer of fabric after all others are cut.

Diagonal pieces should be placed on the bias grain.

marking

Transferring markings from the pattern to your cut pieces is important to ensure the best results.

Center front, back, and matched pivot or clipping marks are the most crucial pattern symbols. Other markings may not require transferring.

There are a variety of tools and techniques used in transferring pattern markings onto fabric. Choose a marking method according to the fabric you are using.

For example, a mark that can only be removed by dampening the fabric, such as a water-soluble or dissolving pen, is unsuitable for dry-clean-only fabric. Tools that make holes, such as a serrated tracing wheel, are not advisable to use on delicate fabrics or leather because the holes will be permanent. In most cases a combination of marking techniques work best. Always test your marking method on a scrap of the actual project fabric. The mark should come off easily without damage.

The garment pieces should be marked after you have cut them out. Keep the pattern pieces in place before moving them from the cutting table. Mark most pattern details on the wrong side of the fabric. The few exceptions are the placement markings for surface details such as patch pockets. Mark both fabric layers unless the marking is intended for one side only, such as a single pocket on a shirt. Buttonholes are marked on one side of the opening and button placements on the corresponding side.

notching

Cutting notches—V-shaped cuts in the seam allowances to indicate centers, front and back armholes or necklines, and the ends of stitching lines—can be a timesaver. Use a pair of scissors that are sharp all the way to the tips.

Fold the fabric at a right angle to the stitching line and snip a small notch out of the seam allowance, ending with the point ³⁄₁₆" from the seam line. This method is not suitable for patterns with narrow seam allowances of ¼" or less.

basting

Thread marking takes the most time but is invaluable for fabrics unsuitable for other forms of marking. Lines of basting can be used to mark the center front or back lines, fold lines, or the roll line of a collar.

Use contrasting thread. Different-colored threads can also be used to distinguish various details. Try to avoid basting along sewing lines because the basting thread may get caught in the stitching. When the position of a design detail, such as a pocket, is required on the right side, trace the position on the wrong side using another marking method; then baste along the marked line to make the marks visible on the front.

tailor's tacks

Isolated points are best marked with a tailor's tack. They are particularly useful to mark the tip and the matching points along the length of a dart. These thread tacks are worked through a tissue paper pattern piece and two layers of fabric beneath, thereby marking both halves of a garment piece.

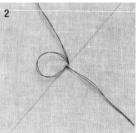

1. Use doubled thread without knotting the end. Take a tiny stitch through the mark on the pattern. Pull the thread through, leaving a 1¼" tail.

2. Take another stitch through the same point and pull through, leaving a 1¼" loop.

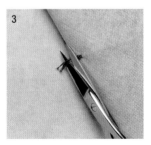

3. Trim the thread, leaving a 1¼" tail. Carefully pull the pattern piece away. Lift the top layer of fabric to the limit of the thread loops. Snip through the threads midway between the layers of fabric.

4. Open out the garment pieces; each piece is tacked.

pressing

Pressing is an essential part of good garment construction. Keep the ironing board with the iron on a low setting ready near your sewing area.

pressing tools

Irons can vary from a simple model to a deluxe ironing system that includes a large water reservoir and suction board. Common problems with irons are scale buildup in the water tank and a soiled sole plate. Using distilled water or buying an iron with a filter can help to alleviate the scale problem. Cleaning the iron regularly will keep the sole plate in good order.

An **ironing board** should be sturdy with a smooth padded cover. Keep the cover clean to prevent marks transferring to the fabric that is being pressed.

A **sleeve board** is a smaller version of an ironing board. It enables you to press tight, narrow sections of garments such as sleeves and cuffs.

A **pressing ham** is a very firmly filled pillow of fabric, usually wool on one side and cotton on the other. A pressing ham is used for pressing small areas that are difficult to reach on a flat surface and for pressing curves and rolling collars.

A **sleeve roll** is cylindrical in shape and similar to a pressing ham. It is particularly useful for pressing sleeves and other parts of a garment that cannot be laid flat.

A **pressing mitt** is a glove-shaped device. The mitt is worn on the hand and pushed into areas that cannot be laid flat.

Pressing cloths are used when steam ironing and are excellent for setting pleats and removing creases. Pieces of plain white cotton fabric are useful for preventing scorching when pressing delicate fabrics, and for protecting your iron from glue when fusing interfacing and appliqué.

Flannel or fine toweling is helpful when pressing embroidery. Fold the cloth into a pad, place it beneath the embroidery, and press the back of the fabric.

Pin boards are invaluable when pressing fabric with a nap, such as corduroy or velvet. They resemble a miniature bed of nails. The fabric is laid face down onto the board and pressed from the back. The pins prevent the nap from being pressed flat.

how to press

Pressing is not the same as ironing. When ironing, you move the iron over the fabric to remove creases. Pressing involves very little movement of the iron and more pressure in certain areas. Use a press-and-lift action rather than gliding over the fabric. Move the iron in the general direction of the straight grain wherever possible.

Pattern instructions will tell you when to press, but as a general rule, press each seam or section before it is crossed by another.

Press on the wrong side or use a pressing cloth to protect the right side from iron shine.

When attaching two different-colored fabrics, press the seam allowances toward the darker of the two wherever possible. The dark fabric will conceal the seam allowances on the right side. If this is not possible, grade the darker seam allowance so it is more narrow than the lighter one.

If several seams meet at the same point, aim to press all seam allowances open rather than to one side. This will reduce bulk on the wrong side at the junction.

troubleshooting

Type	Problem	Solution
Machine	Machine working, but the flywheel isn't turning	• The bobbin case and hook area may be jammed with lint or thread. Pull the bobbin and case out of the hook-assembly bed and rock the flywheel back and forth gently while pulling on the thread. Clean out any crevices using the accessory brush.
	Needle doesn't move	• The needle may still be disengaged from the last time you wound a bobbin. • If the needle is engaged, the flywheel belt may be slipping because it's loose or worn.
	Machine and needle working, but the fabric isn't feeding through	• Check to make sure that the presser foot is down and the foot is clamped tight. • The stitch length regulator may be set at 0. • The pressure regulator may be at 0 or in the free-motion position. • The feed dogs may be lowered.
Stitching	Stitch length is uneven	• Pulling or pushing the fabric through will cause this. • The pressure regulator might be set too heavy or too light for the fabric.
	Loops are forming on the right or wrong side	• The top thread is incorrectly threaded or tensioned, causing loops to form on the wrong side causing loops to for on the right side. • The bobbin is unevenly wound, incorrectly threaded, or not seated in the bobbin case correctly, causing loops to form on the right side.
	Skipping stitches	• Problems with the needle are the most common cause. It may be blunt or bent, inserted incorrectly, or the housing not clamped tight enough. • The needle may be the wrong type for the fabric. • There may be insufficient pressure on the presser foot.
	Wide stitches pulling in the fabric	• The tension is too tight. • Less tension is needed for zigzag and embroidery stitches. • The fabric may be too sheer—stabilize with spray starch or place interfacing underneath.
Tension	Adjustments don't last	• Tension discs may have worn loose over time—they are replaceable. • Reduce wear on the discs by not pulling the thread through while the presser foot is raised.
Fabric	Layers feed unevenly	• Pressure regulator is too light or too heavy. Stitch more slowly and increase the tension on the upper layer with your hands as you feed the fabric through. • Stabilize lightweight or slippery fabrics with spray starch to increase the surface tension or use tearaway stabilizer on top of or under the fabric when stitching.
	Stitching puckers the fabric	• The needle and thread may be unsuitable for the fabric. • The stitch tension may be unbalanced. • Stitching will usually pucker a single layer of fabric unless it has been stabilized.
Thread	Tangling underneath at the beginning of a seam	• This can be prevented by placing the needle into the fabric before beginning to stitch. Hold both threads at the back until a few stitches have been formed; then let go.
	Thread and fabric has been pushed into the stitch plate hole	• Rock the flywheel back and forth while gently pulling on the fabric to release the tangle. Snip the threads and pull out any loose ends. Start the stitching again.

appliqué

Appliqué is a French term meaning "to apply." The simplest form of appliqué is worked by stitching cut fabric shapes to a base fabric, forming a design or pattern. A design with simple shapes works best. Details can be added using embroidery or embellishment such as beads or buttons after the basic shapes have been attached. Almost any fabric is suitable for appliqué, but as a general rule, choose smooth, densely woven fabric for the background and lightweight fabrics with similar laundering properties for the design shapes. Appliqué may be stitched by machine or by hand, depending on the effect you wish to achieve.

Fused and hand-stitched appliqué

before you start

1. Launder the fabrics to remove the sizing and any chemical residue. This will ensure that the fabrics bond properly.

2. If the base fabric is lightweight or stretchy, stabilize it with interfacing to provide a firm base for stitching.

3. Appliqué by hand or machine may be done in a hoop to prevent the base fabric from puckering or distorting.

4. Aim to match the grain of the appliqué pieces with that of the base fabric wherever possible.

hints
hand appliqué

While machine stitching secures the raw edges of the pieced fabric, hand stitching is not as dense. It may be necessary to turn under a seam allowance on the pieces to hide the raw edges.

Fusible web makes the pieced fabric less likely to fray, so turning under a seam allowance isn't always crucial.

fusible appliqué

Fusible web, used to bond fabric pieces together, has made preparing and stitching appliqué much easier than more traditional methods. The shapes are traced onto the smooth side of the fusible web's paper backing as a mirror image to ensure correct orientation when attached to the base fabric. The internal design lines defining each element can be stitched as if they are separate pieces of fabric.

Read the manufacturer's instructions carefully before you start using fusible products and ensure the fabrics you choose are compatible with the heat setting required for the product.

Choose a design and simplify the shapes within it if necessary. Consider the colors you wish to use and collect pieces of fabric to suit.

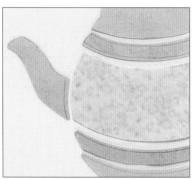

1. Trace the design onto paper using a permanent pen. Tape the tracing over a light source. Place the base fabric over the design, right side up. Using a sharp lead pencil, trace the design outline only onto the fabric.

2. Reposition the tracing over the light source with the reverse side up. Place fusible web over the tracing with the smooth side up. Trace the individual elements, grouped according to the fabrics used.

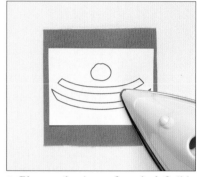

3. Place each piece of marked fusible web with the rough side down on the appropriate fabric. Position the iron firmly in the center of the paper for a few seconds before moving it around to fuse the piece.

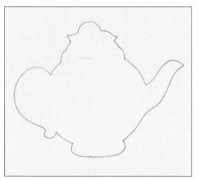

4. Allow the pieces to cool. Cut out the elements, leaving a small seam allowance on any edges that will be covered by an adjacent shape.

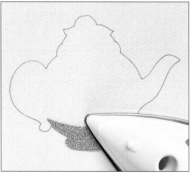

5. Remove the paper backing. Begin with the elements layered beneath adjacent areas. Position them right side up and fuse in place.

6. Continue to build the design, layering the elements to secure the raw edges. Draw the internal design lines, such as the rim of the lid here, using a fabric marker.

machine appliqué

It is essential to use an open-toe embroidery presser foot on the machine. This foot has a groove underneath that glides easily over the ridge of decorative stitching, and the open front enables you to see where you are sewing. For satin stitching, work with a very close zigzag stitch in a width appropriate to the scale of the design.

hints machine appliqué

Machine stitching is usually worked in sewing thread to match the appliqué fabric; however, contrasting thread adds another dimension.

If you are stitching around an entire shape, trim the thread ends at the beginning. When you reach the starting point, work over the stitching for a short distance. To secure the remaining thread ends, pull the threads to the wrong side and tie off.

1. Position the work under the presser foot with the needle slightly to the right of the edge of an appliqué shape. Stitch along the edge, allowing the needle to enter the shape on the left and just clear it on the right.

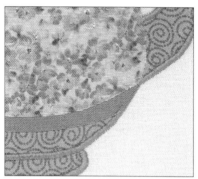

2. **Stitching order.** Stitch around each element, starting and finishing so the ends will be covered by subsequent stitching.

3. Stitch the edges of the remaining elements in the same manner. Press carefully on the wrong side.

turning corners and curves

1. **Outside corners.** Stitch to the corner point, stopping with the needle down on the right-hand side. Lift the presser foot. Pivot the fabric so that the next edge is ready to stitch.

2. **Inside corners.** Stitch into the corner the same distance as the stitch width. Stop with the needle down on the left-hand side. Lift the presser foot. Pivot the fabric and continue as before.

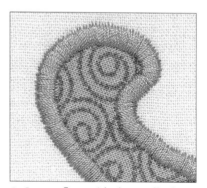

3. **Curves.** Stop with the needle down on the outside of the curve. Lift the presser foot and slightly rotate the fabric into the curve; then continue. The tighter the curve, the more frequently you will need to stop.

appliqué

armholes

bound armhole

This method is used for finishing the raw edge of the armhole on a sleeveless garment. The binding may be made from the same fabric or a contrasting fabric. Because the armhole is curved, the binding should be cut on the true bias, following the instructions on page 39.

single binding

Stitch and press the shoulder and side seams of the bodice. Finish the seams referring to page 126. Determine the desired finished width of the binding. Cut a bias strip to fit around each armhole, cutting it four times the desired finished width and adding twice the width of the binding to the length. The binding will be attached using the same seam allowance as the finished width.

Example: For a ⅜"-wide finished binding, cut the bias strip 1½" wide and 1½" longer than the armhole measurement.

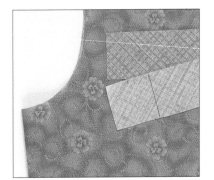

1. Mark a square the same width as the binding on the wrong side of the bias-binding strip at the left-hand end. Mark the upper raw edge in the center of the square.

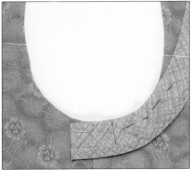

2. Press under the seam allowance on the lower raw edge of the binding. With right sides together and the center mark aligned with the side seam, pin the binding around the armhole.

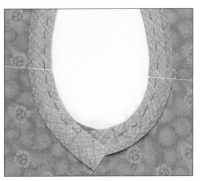

3. As you near the side seam, mark the upper edge of the binding as before to match the side seam. Measure and mark a square with the mark at the center. Trim any excess binding.

4. Remove a few pins and join the ends of the binding following steps 3 and 4 on page 41. Repin and tack the binding in place. Stitch the binding in place around the armhole.

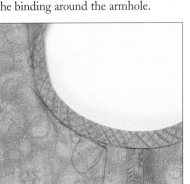

5. Fold the binding to the wrong side and hand stitch in place to cover the stitching line.

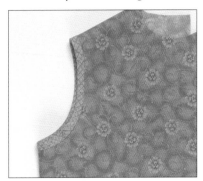

6. Press the binding carefully.

double binding

In this method, the binding is made with a double layer, providing a firmer bound edge.

Preparation

Stitch and press the shoulder and side seams of the bodice. Finish the seams referring to page 126. Determine the desired finished width of the binding.

Cut a bias strip to fit around each armhole, cutting it six times the finished width and adding the width of the binding to the length. The binding will be attached using the same width seam allowance as the finished width of the binding.

Example: For a ⅜"-wide finished binding, cut the bias strip 2¼" wide and 2¼" longer than the armhole measurement.

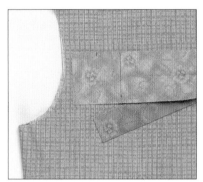

1. Fold the binding in half lengthwise and press. Open the right end. Mark a square the same width as the binding on the wrong side.

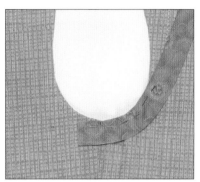

2. Refold the binding. Mark the upper raw edge in the center of the square. Aligning the mark with the side seam and matching the raw edges, pin the binding around the armhole.

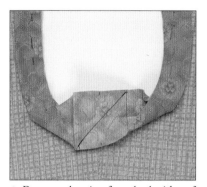

3. Remove the pins from both sides of the side seam. Join the ends of the binding following steps 3 and 4 on page 41. Trim the seam allowances and press open.

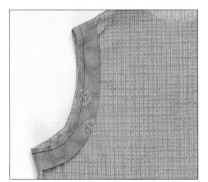

4. Refold the binding and stitch it in place around the armhole.

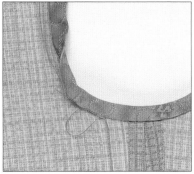

5. Fold the binding to the wrong side and hand stitch in place, covering the stitching.

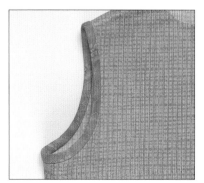

6. Press the binding carefully.

faced armhole

Preparation

Cut the facings using the appropriate pattern pieces or draft your own referring to the instructions on page 80. If any adjustments are made to the armhole edge, make sure to alter the facing piece too. Apply interfacing to the wrong side of the facing pieces.

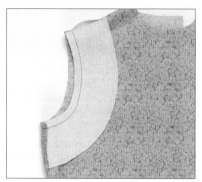

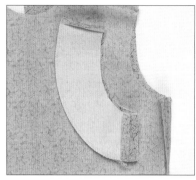

1. Stay stitch around the bodice armhole edges. Stitch and press the shoulder and side seams. Finish seams. Join the facing pieces. Trim the seam allowances and press open. Finish the outer edge of the facing.

2. With right sides together and matching seams, pin the facing to the armhole. Beginning stitching before the side seam, stitch around the armhole, then overstitch the seam for a short distance.

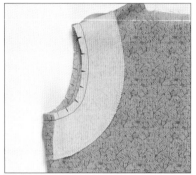

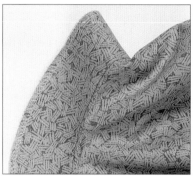

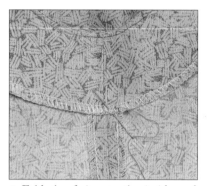

3. Trim the seam allowances to ¼" and clip the curves.

4. Press the facing and facing seam allowances away from the bodice. Understitch around the armhole on the facing about ⅛" from the seam allowances.

5. Fold the facing to the inside and press. Matching seams, hand stitch the facing to the shoulder and side seam allowances only.

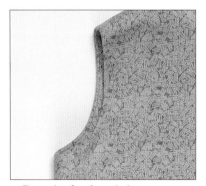

6. Press the faced armhole.

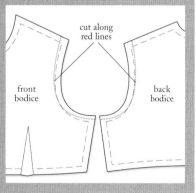

hint altering armholes for binding

If using a pattern not specifically designed for bound armholes, cut away the seam allowances on the armhole edge.

Note that if the armhole was designed for a set-in sleeve, it will be deeper than necessary or the shoulder line might extend beyond the top of the arm. Trimming away less at the underarm and more at the shoulder should result in a better fit.

cut along red lines

front bodice

back bodice

belts

Belts can take a multitude of forms and although they can be viewed as a decorative fashion element, they are also practical. Except for soft tie belts, most belts need some form of reinforcing. Shaped belts should be made with a heavier-weight interfacing such as buckram. For straight belts, the fabric is stretched taut around a special strip of belt stiffening to give a firm finish.

tie belt

Preparation

Cut a piece of fabric long enough to fit comfortably around the body at the desired position, adding extra length for the knot and ties. Cut fabric twice the desired width, plus seam allowances on both long edges. Mark the center of the long edges.

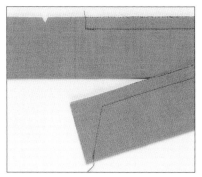 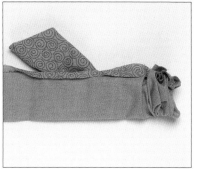 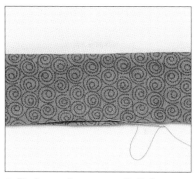

1. Fold the fabric right sides together, matching the raw edges, and pin. Beginning 1" from the center mark, stitch along the raw edge. Pivot at the corner, stitch across the end, and secure.

2. Return to the center and stitch the remaining half in the same manner, leaving a 2" opening for turning. Clip the corners and turn the belt to the right side through the opening.

3. Push out the corners. Roll the seam to the edge and press, pressing the folded seam allowances across the opening. Hand stitch the opening closed using ladder stitch (page 88). Press.

straight belt

The instructions on the following page show a self-covered buckle, but any buckle the same width as the belt stiffening may be used. If the buckle has no prong, wrap the raw end of the belt around the bar in the middle and secure in the same manner as in step 7 on page 36. Eyelets are not required for this type of buckle but the carrier should be added.

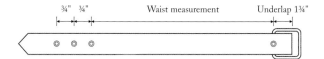

¾" ¾"   Waist measurement   Underlap 1¾"

Preparation

Cut a strip of belt stiffening to fit comfortably around the waist plus 8". Trim one end to a shallow point. Cut the fabric ¾" longer and twice the width of the stiffening, adding a ³⁄₈" seam allowance on each long edge. Make a carrier that is the width of the belt plus ¾", following steps 1 and 2 on page 37.

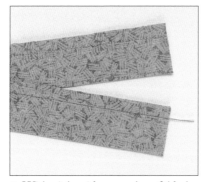

1. With right sides together, fold the fabric in half along the length and pin. Stitch the long edges using a ³⁄₈" seam allowance.

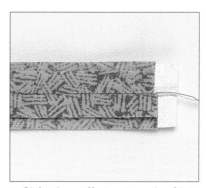

2. Slide the stiffening into the fabric tube, ensuring it fits tightly. Move the seam to the center and press open.

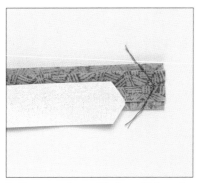

3. Remove the stiffening. Using the end of the stiffening as a template, mark the point on the fabric ¼" back from one end. Stitch the point. Trim, leaving a ¼" seam allowance.

4. Turn the fabric tube right side out. Slide the stiffening back into the tube until the pointed end is snug. Smooth out the fabric and press.

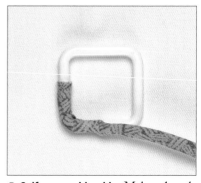

5. Self-covered buckle. Make a length of bias-cut ¼" tubing long enough to cover the buckle, adding extra to neaten the ends. Slide the tubing onto the buckle at the slotted opening.

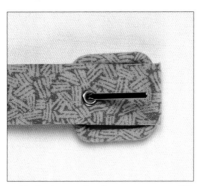

6. Referring to the diagram on page 35, add grommets to the belt following the manufacturer's instructions. Place the prong of the buckle from the wrong side through the grommet at the raw end of the belt.

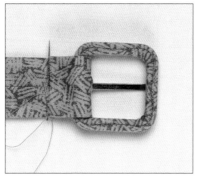

7. Wrong side. Take the underlap through the buckle, wrapping it around the bar. Fold under the raw end. Hand or machine stitch to secure.

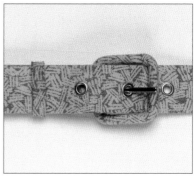

8. Wrap the carrier around the belt, allowing room for the belt to slide through. Folding one raw end under, overlap the ends, and hand stitch to secure.

belts

36

belt loops

To ensure belts stay at the desired position on a garment, they are usually held in place by belt loops inserted into the side seams or attached to waistbands.

fabric belt loop

This type of belt loop can be set into the side seams or waistband.

Preparation

Cut lengths of fabric four times the finished width of the belt loop and long enough to suit the width of the belt or waistband, adding seam allowances. It is easier to make one long strip and cut it into individual lengths.

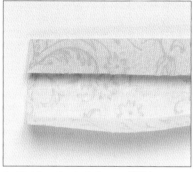

1. Making the belt loops. With wrong sides together, fold the strip in half lengthwise and press. Unfold. Fold the raw edges to meet at the center fold line and press.

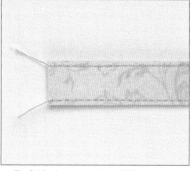

2. Refold the strip in half lengthwise, enclosing the raw edges. Topstitch along both long edges.

3. Attaching to waistband. Prepare the waistband and facing. Matching raw edges, position the belt loop on the waistband. Baste in place just inside the seam allowance.

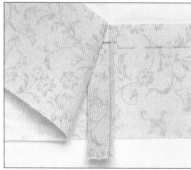

4. With right sides together and matching raw edges, pin and stitch the waistband and facing along the upper edge, sandwiching the belt loop between.

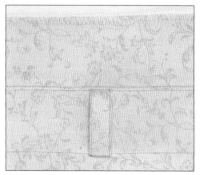

5. Trim the seam allowances and press toward the facing. Understitch. Attach the lower edge of the waistband to the garment, sandwiching the remaining end of the belt loop in the seam.

6. Alternatively, attach the waistband to the garment leaving the raw end of the belt loop free. Secure the facing. Turn under the raw end of the belt loop and machine stitch securely in place.

in-seam fabric loop

Preparation

Make a desired length of narrow tubing following the instructions on page 139, adding seam allowances on both ends.

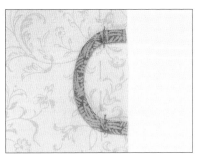

1. On the right side, pin the tube in position on a garment seam, spacing the ends slightly wider than the belt. Baste within the seam allowance.

2. Pin and stitch the two garment pieces together, sandwiching the belt loop between.

3. Finish the seam and press.

chain loop with detached blanket stitch

Use two strands of strong thread such as topstitching or quilting thread. Cut long lengths to avoid having to join new thread.

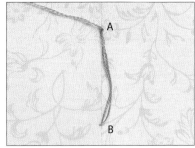

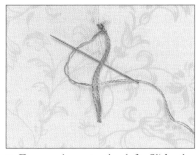

1. Secure the thread on the wrong side. Bring it to the front at A. Leaving a loose straight stitch, work several tiny backstitches at B. Return to A and secure the second long stitch as before.

2. Form a loop to the left. Slide the needle from right to left under the straight stitches and over the loop.

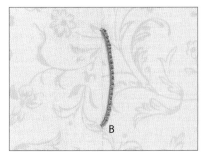

3. Pull the thread through, forming a snug stitch. Form a loop to the right. Slide the needle from left to right under the stitches and over the loop.

4. Finish the stitch as before. Continue alternating the blanket stitches for the length of the loop. Take the thread to the back at B and secure.

binding

Binding is a strip of fabric folded over the raw edge of the project from one side to the other to conceal and finish raw edges. It's a practical way to prevent edges from fraying and it provides a decorative edge. It's generally the same width on the front as it is on the back. To bind a curved edge, use binding cut on the bias. This will allow it to fit the curve without twisting or puckering. Straight edges cut on the straight of grain can be bound with tape, ribbon, braid, or fabric strips cut on grain.

cutting bias binding

For the best result, cut bias binding on the true bias, on a 45° angle to the selvage edge.

Preparation

The most accurate way to find the true bias is to pull a thread on both the lengthwise and crosswise grain, then fold the fabric to match the pulled thread lines. The diagonal fold created is the true bias—at a 45° angle to the selvage edge.

cutting strips

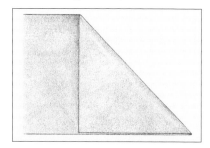

1. Press the fold and then open the fabric. Measure from the fold line and mark the width of the binding you wish to cut.

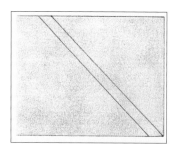

2. Cut strips on the marked lines. Leave the ends of the strips tapered or trim them at a right angle to the edge of the strip, depending on personal preference or the technique being used.

cutting continuous bias

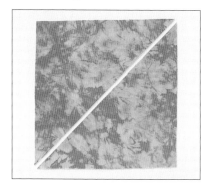

1. Cut a large square of fabric. Fold it diagonally in half and press the fold. Unfold and cut the fabric along the fold line.

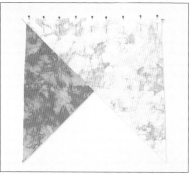

2. With right sides together, place the two triangles so that the edges meet along one short side of each triangle and the long sides are at right angles. Pin.

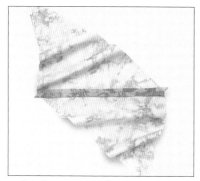

3. Stitch, using a ¼" seam allowance. Press the seam allowances open.

4. Decide the width of bias strip you need. Using a ruler, mark lines across the fabric parallel to the bias edge, keeping them evenly spaced at the required measurement.

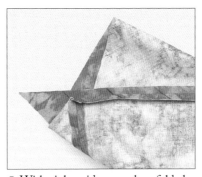

5. With rights sides together, fold the fabric so the diagonal ends meet. Offset the ends so the first line on one edge is aligned with the edge of the fabric.

6. Pin the ends, so that the marked lines match at the seam line.

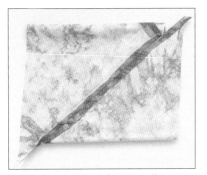

7. Stitch using a ¼" seam allowance. Press the seam allowances open.

8. Turn right side out. Beginning at one offset end, cut along the marked line through one layer of fabric only.

joining bias binding

When joining lengths of bias binding, the seam should cross the binding diagonally or the binding won't stretch at this point. A diagonal seam is less visible than a straight one.

Joining straight ends

1. Matching raw edges, place the ends of the bias strips perpendicular to one another, right sides together, and pin. Mark a line between the upper right and lower left corners. Stitch along the marked line.

2. Trim the excess fabric, leaving a ¼" seam allowance. Press seam allowances open.

Joining diagonal ends

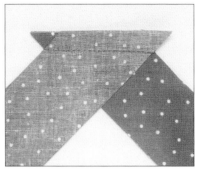

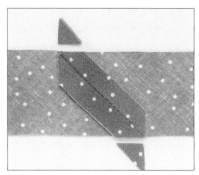

1. On the wrong side, mark a ¼" seam allowance across the ends of both strips. Place the ends right sides together, aligning the marked lines. Stitch across the end.

2. Press the seam allowances open and trim the points.

Joining ends to form a continuous binding

This method is used when a continuous binding is required, such as a bound armhole or the outer edge of a pillow or quilt. For bias binding, the join should follow the grain of the fabric across the diagonal to give a fine finish and ensure strength and flexibility. Binding cut on the straight grain can be joined with a straight seam.

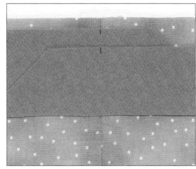

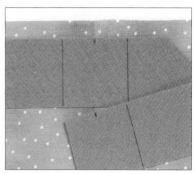

1. Leaving excess binding on both ends, pin the binding around the edge to be bound. Mark the upper edge of both ends at the center point for the join.

2. Measure half the width of the binding on either side of the center marks and draw lines at right angles to the edge across the binding to form squares. Trim excess binding.

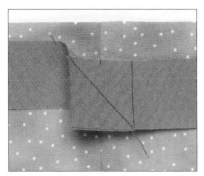

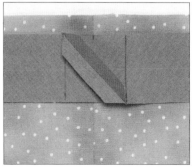

3. Mark a line between the upper-left and lower-right corners on the right-hand end of the binding strip. Place the ends of the binding right sides together, with ends perpendicular to one another, and pin. Stitch along the marked line.

4. Trim the seam allowance and press open.

applying binding

If your project has a seam allowance on the edge that you want to bind, trim it away before attaching the binding. The following examples can be stitched using binding cut on the bias or straight grain. Method one is the most commonly used, but method two is most appropriate for transparent fabrics. For either method, to determine the width of the binding strip, decide on the finished width and multiply this by four. The width of the seam allowance is the same as the width of the binding.

Single binding, method 1

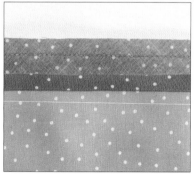

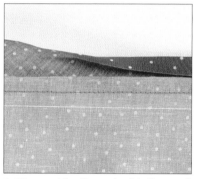

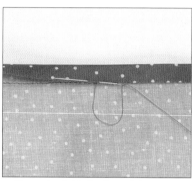

1. Press under the seam allowance along one long raw edge of the binding. With right sides together and matching raw edges, pin and stitch the unfolded edge of the binding.

2. Wrong side. Press the binding and seam allowances away from the garment.

3. Turn the folded edge of the binding to the wrong side, enclosing the seam allowances. Pin and hand stitch the fold to the stitching line.

Single binding, method 2

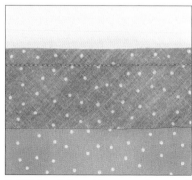

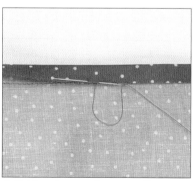

1. With right sides together and matching raw edges, pin and stitch the binding in place.

2. Wrong side. Press the binding away from the garment edge and the seam allowances toward the garment. Fold the remaining raw edge of the binding to meet the stitching line and press the fold.

3. Fold and press the seam allowances over the raw edge of the binding. Fold the pressed binding to the wrong side enclosing the seam. Hand stitch along the previous stitching line.

double-fold binding or french binding

Preparation

To determine the width of the binding strip for this method, decide on the finished width and multiply this by six. The width of the seam allowance is the same as the width of the binding.

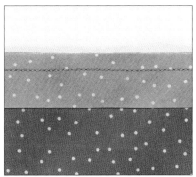

1. Fold the binding strip in half lengthwise and press. With right sides together and matching raw edges, pin and stitch.

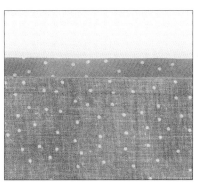

2. Wrong side. Press the binding and seam allowances away from the garment.

3. Fold the pressed edge to the wrong side, enclosing the seam allowances. Pin and hand stitch the fold to the previous stitching line.

quick binding

This method is essentially the same as the previous methods except that the binding is secured by machine stitching. Any binding can be secured by machine, either with topstitching or the method known as "stitch in the ditch," as long as the binding has been wrapped over the seam allowances with the fold covering the previous stitching line. The example on page 99 shows a bound neckline using purchased bias binding.

hints binding

A rotary cutter is handy for cutting bias and straight-grain binding.

Stretch bias binding very slightly as you pin it in place along concave curves, such as armholes and necklines. This will give a smoother result.

After stitching the binding in place, take care not to trim away too much of the seam allowances. Enough should remain to fill the width of the binding, making it firm, smooth, and less likely to buckle along the outer edge.

button bands

Button bands create a tailored finish to the front opening edges of a shirt, jacket, or skirt. The center front of the garment runs down the middle of the band. Depending on the weight of the fabric, lightweight interfacing should be applied to one or both layers of the band to provide stability for the buttons and buttonholes.

Preparation

Before attaching the band, stitch the hem on the lower edge of the garment. Apply interfacing to the wrong side of the button bands as required. Ensure you have a left and right band.

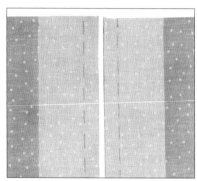

1. Press under the seam allowances on the long raw edge of the non-inter-faced half and trim to ¼".

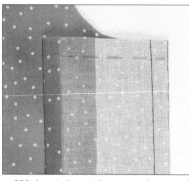

2. With right sides together and matching raw edges, pin and stitch the long raw edge of the band to the edge of the garment. Align the upper end with the raw edge of the neckline.

3. Trim the seam allowance to ¼". The lower end of the band should extend past the garment hem by the width of the seam allowance.

4. Press the band away from the garment. At the lower end, fold the band right sides together, aligning the long folded edge with the seam line. Stitch across the end of the band.

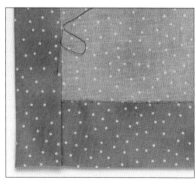

5. Trim the seam allowances. Turn the band to the right side at the lower end and carefully push out the corner. On the wrong side, align the folded edge with the stitching line. Pin and hand stitch in place.

buttonholes

Standard buttonholes, horizontal or vertical, consist of two parallel rows of close machine zigzag stitching with a bartack at each end. Some may have a rounded or keyhole end where the button sits. Buttonholes have to withstand a lot of strain when a garment is worn, so adding interfacing between the fabric layers behind the buttonholes will help to stabilize and strengthen the fabric.

Placement

Horizontal buttonholes are stitched at a right angle to the center front or back line, with the first bartack just past the center.

Vertical buttonholes follow the center line, centered over the button position.

To ensure that an opening on a garment closes accurately, the buttonholes and the corresponding buttons must align correctly.

Pattern pieces will indicate the placement of any buttonholes required and these should be transferred to the fabric piece as part of the pattern markings. Buttonholes are usually marked as a line with a small bar at one or both ends. The line indicates the length of the buttonhole after it is cut. The bartacks at the ends should begin at the bars, not cover them.

The length of a buttonhole should equal the diameter plus the thickness of the button being used. If you have decided on a button wider or narrower than those specified in the pattern, alter the position of the bartack on the far end of the buttonhole rather than the front end on horizontal buttonholes. The front end is where the button sits and is positioned to close the opening with the correct overlap.

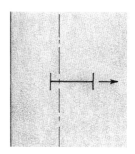

For vertical buttonholes, the length should be altered evenly at both ends.

hint horizontal or vertical buttonholes

Generally, a buttonhole is placed perpendicular to the edge of the opening. Button bands are an exception. They should always contain vertical buttonholes parallel to the edge.

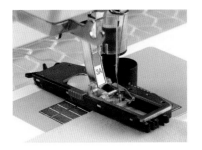

machine-stitched buttonholes

Depending on what type of sewing maching you have, you will be able to make semi- or fully automatic buttonholes. If your machine has a fully automatic buttonhole presser foot, a button is placed in the back of the foot and the machine gauges the correct buttonhole length to fit. If the button is particularly thick, add extra length to allow for the thickness, following the instructions in your machine manual.

For semi-automatic buttonholes, use the buttonhole foot and the preset buttonhole settings on your machine to work a buttonhole at the marked position, following the instructions in your manual. The following instructions will aid you in positioning buttonholes on unmarked openings or if you have altered the spacing or placement away from the buttonhole template provided in a pattern.

Vertical buttonholes

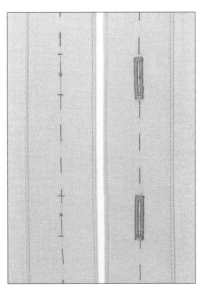

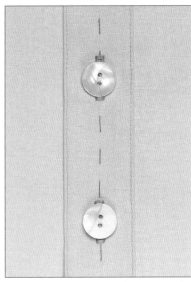

1. Mark the button positions following steps 1 and 2 for horizontal buttonholes, opposite, placing the upper and lower dots half the button width plus ½"–⅝" from the edge.

2. Stitch the buttonholes using the preferred method and attach the buttons at the marked positions.

Horizontal buttonholes

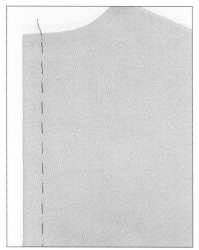

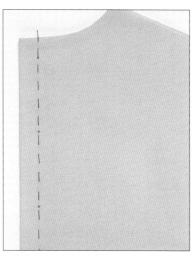

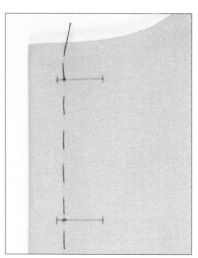

1. Determine the center front or back position from the pattern piece. Baste a line between the upper and lower center points. Alternatively, mark a line using a suitable fabric marker and ruler.

2. Measure from the upper edge half the button width plus ³⁄₁₆"–¼" and mark on the tacked line. Repeat at the bottom edge. Divide the distance between the marks by the number of buttons minus one. Mark each point.

3. Beginning ⅛" away from the dot toward the opening edge, mark the length of a horizontal buttonhole. Move the starting point slightly forward if the button has a thick shank.

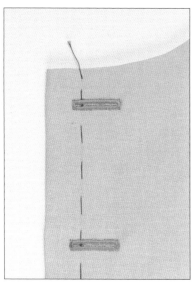

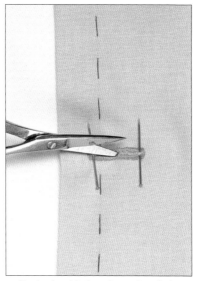

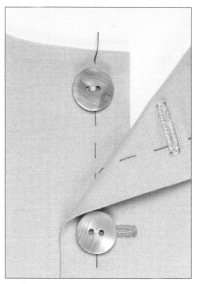

4. Stitch the buttonholes at the marked positions using the machine settings.

5. Push the blade of a pair of sharp pointed scissors into the center of the buttonhole and snip toward the ends. To prevent the bartacks from being cut, place pins through the ends of the buttonhole.

6. Centering each button on a marked dot, attach the buttons following the instructions on pages 54–56.

bound buttonholes

Bound buttonholes are a neat, tailored alternative to a stitched opening. To ensure uniformity, complete the same step on all the buttonholes before moving to the next step.

Preparation

Mark the position for the buttonhole on the right side of the fabric. Mark a line ⅛" on either side of the marked line (increase to ¼" for thick fabrics). Extend the center line and end bars. Cut a patch of fabric 2⅜" wide and 1" longer than the finished opening. Apply interfacing and draw the markings on the wrong side of the patch. With right sides together and matching the lines, center the patch over the marked buttonhole and pin in place.

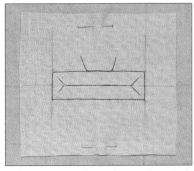

1. Using a small stitch length, stitch around the marked rectangle. Pivot at the corners and overlap the beginning stitches. Snip along the center line and clip diagonally into each corner. Do not cut through the stitching.

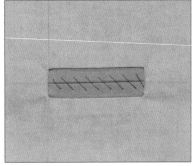

3. Repeat step 2 on the top edge of the opening. Adjust the pleats to ensure the binding is even on both edges. Tack the edges together with thread. Pin the pleats together on the wrong side.

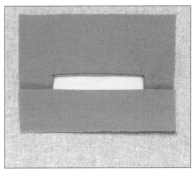

2. Wrong side. Pull the patch through to the wrong side of the garment and adjust the opening to form a rectangle. Press. Fold a pleat in the bottom of the patch, aligning the fold with the center of the opening.

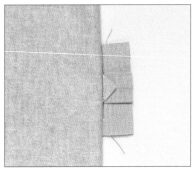

4. With the right side facing up, fold the garment edge over to expose one end of the patch. Stitch across the end. Repeat at the remaining end.

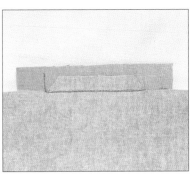

5. Repeat step 4 on the upper and lower edges of the opening, stitching just inside the original stitching line. Trim the excess fabric around the outer edge of the patch and press.

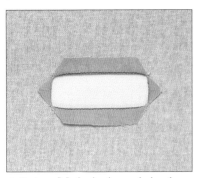

6. Facing. Mark the buttonhole placement on the facing piece. Stay stitch around the opening. Clip along the center and ends as before. Press the seam allowances to the wrong side of the facing.

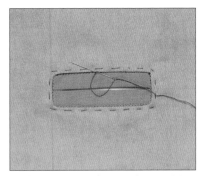

7. With wrong sides together, position the prepared facing over the back of the buttonhole and baste in place. Hand stitch to secure and remove the basting.

hand-stitched buttonholes

Working buttonholes by hand can add a special touch to a garment. They are particularly suited to delicate fabrics such as organdy or batiste, but they can be worked on most garments. Mark the buttonhole on the fabric, adding extra lines to mark the width. Cut the opening.

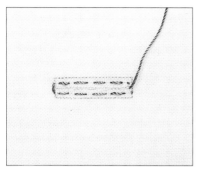

1. Work running stitches around the buttonhole, finishing at the right-hand end. Bring the thread to the front through the opening.

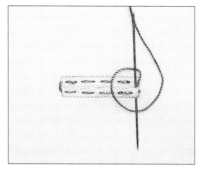

2. Take the needle through the opening and emerge on the lower line. Wrap the thread counterclockwise behind the eye end, and then the tip of the needle.

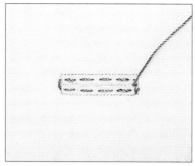

3. Pull the thread through, bringing it toward you and then up toward the opening, until the knot settles on the cut edge.

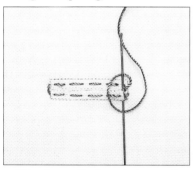

4. Take the needle through the opening again and emerge next to the previous stitch. Wrap the thread around the needle as before.

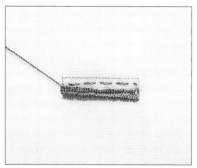

5. Continue in this manner until you reach the end of the opening. Keep the stitches as close together as possible.

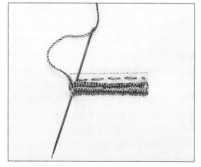

6. Bartack. Take the needle through the opening and emerge close to the previous stitch on the lower line.

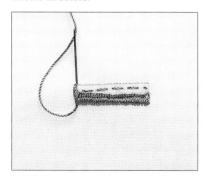

7. Work several stitches across the end. Take the needle to the back at the upper edge.

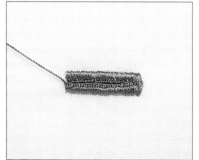

8. Turn the fabric upside down. Work the buttonhole stitch as before across the remaining long edge.

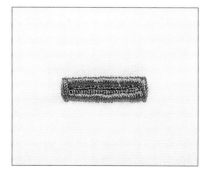

9. Make a bartack as in steps 6 and 7. Take the thread through to the back, weave it through the stitching, and trim.

button loops

Button loops provide a decorative closure, often used for the opening of wedding gowns where the finished edge of the opening is on the center back. Shank or ball buttons are particularly suited for this type of closure.

Button loops are also a decorative way to hold the buttons on a sleeve cuff or pocket tab instead of a plain stitched buttonhole.

For a fabric loop, make a test length to see if the fabric is suitable. Alternatively, use a length of narrow cord for the loops. Attach a button onto a scrap piece of fabric to determine the size of loop needed to slip snugly over the button. This will ensure that it holds the fabric edges together securely in the correct position.

single button loop

The instructions shown are for attaching a button loop for a back neckline closure, but could be adapted to other uses. (See the "Hints" box below.)

It is often easier to attach the lining or facing to the neckline before continuing on to the back opening.

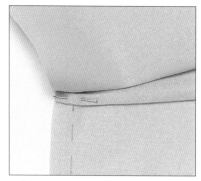

1. Mark the back opening stitching line. Make a length of tubing following the instructions on page 139.

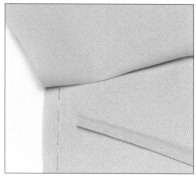

2. Matching raw edges and with the tube seam at the lower edge, pin one end of the tube just below the neck opening seam line.

(See the instructions on page 139.)

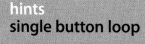

hints
single button loop

There are many other uses for fabric loops such as;

- a closure for a patch pocket or bag
- a hanging loop for an oven mitt or pot holder
- a decorative alternative to a buttonhole on a narrow sleeve band.

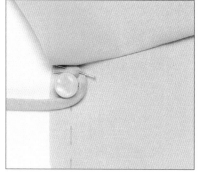

3. Center the button on the seam line just below the tube. Wrap the tube around the button, positioning the edge just under the button.

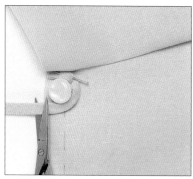

4. Trim the remaining end of the tube even with the raw edge of the garment.

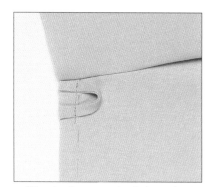

5. Pin the lower end of the tube in place. Remove the button and baste the tube to the garment just inside the seam allowance.

6. Pin and stitch the facing over the garment piece, sandwiching the loop in between.

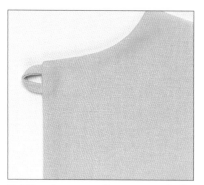

7. Trim the seam allowances and clip the corner. Turn the garment right side out and press, avoiding the loop. Sew button to left back.

continuous loops

Multiple loops can be formed directly onto the garment as described for a single loop. Depending on the size of the buttons, the loops can be placed side by side or spaced further apart. The smaller the buttons, the closer together they should be to close the garment effectively.

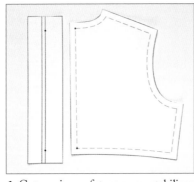

1. Cut a piece of tear-away stabilizer longer than the back opening and 2⅜" wide. Mark the center back dots. Mark a second line ¼" to the left of the first.

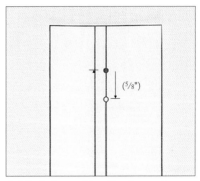

2. Mark the position for the top button on the first line, ⅝" from the top. Repeat at the lower end.

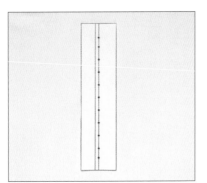

3. Divide the distance between the marks by the number of buttons less one and mark these positions.

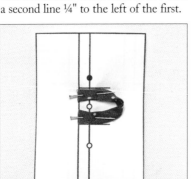

4. Aligning the raw ends with the second line, pin a length of tubing at the top button position following step 3 of the single loop (page 51). Mark the edge above and below and remove the tubing.

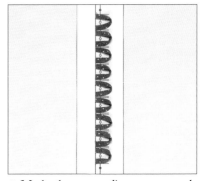

5. Mark the same distances at each button position. Cut strips of tubing for each button. Pin a length at each position, aligning the marks. Baste the tubing to the tear-away template.

6. Matching center lines, place the template on the right side of the back opening with the loops facing into the garment. Baste the loops in place and then tear away the template.

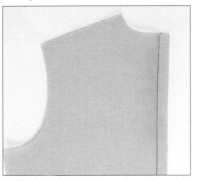

7. With right sides together, place the facing or lining over the loops. Pin together horizontally and stitch just inside the basting.

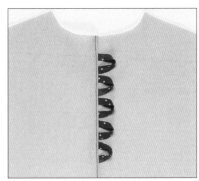

8. Trim the seam allowances and press the facing and seam allowances away from the garment. Understitch along the facing as shown. When complete, press the facing to the wrong side, taking care to avoid the loops.

purchased loop tape

Cut a length of the tape to fit the opening, plus two extra loops. Pull out one loop at each end, leaving the tails of the elastic cord.

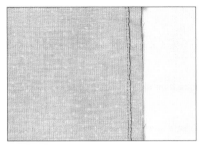

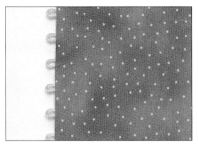

1. With the loops facing inward, position the edge of the tape just inside the stitching line. Fold the excess tape at the ends into the seam allowance. Baste along the edge of the tape, securing the tails.

2. With right sides together, place the facing or lining over the loops. Pin and stitch just inside the basting.

3. Press the facing and seam allowances away from the garment. Understitch along the facing as shown in step 8, opposite.

thread loop

When a front or back button closure is fastened correctly, a small flap of the bodice will extend beyond the first button. Attaching a tiny button and thread loop adds the perfect finishing touch. Use doubled thread in a color to match the fabric. The distance between A and B should be slightly less than the width of the button. Alternating the direction of the blanket stitches will prevent the loop from twisting.

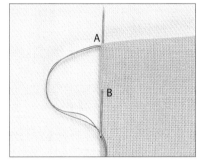

1. Bring the thread to the front through the top seam at A. Make a few tiny stitches to secure the thread. Slide the needle between the fabric layers from B to A.

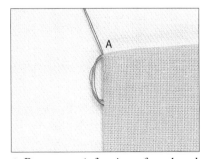

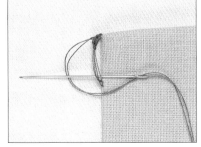

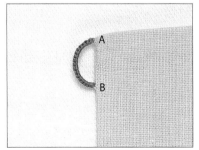

2. Repeat step 1, forming a four-thread loop. Test the size of the loop with the button and adjust if necessary. Secure the thread at A with a few tiny stitches.

3. Work detached blanket stitches around the thread loop. (See page 38.) For every other stitch, work the blanket stitch in the opposite direction.

4. Work blanket stitches alternating from side to side, pulling firmly toward A. When the loop is covered, secure the thread at B.

buttons

The method of attaching a button depends on the style of the button.

Preparation

Mark the positions for the buttons after the buttonholes have been stitched and cut open.

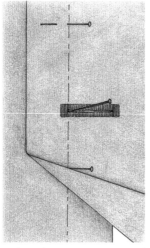

1. Overlap the two sections of the garment, aligning the center lines. Place a pin through the buttonhole and into the underlap.

2. Ease the pin through the buttonhole without removing it from the fabric. Mark the button position on the center line level with the pin.

attaching buttons by machine

Machine stitching is a quick way to sew on buttons, especially if you have to attach a great number. Because the stitching can be easily unraveled, the thread ends should be finished by hand. Mark the center line and the position of the buttons with tacking at right angles to each other. Stitch the buttons in place following the instructions in your manual. Here a toothpick is used to create a thread shank. See more about this, opposite.

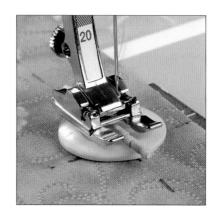

hand stitching flat buttons

When the button is attached, it's a good idea to create a thread shank behind the button, especially on thicker fabrics. This allows the overlapping fabric to fit under the button without causing puckering. The thicker the fabric, the longer the shank needs to be.

A matchstick or toothpick can be used as a spacer when creating the shank. If you don't use a spacer, keep the stitches loose but even.

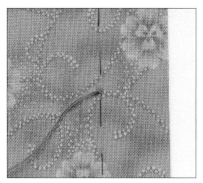

1. Two-hole button. Mark the position for the button on the fabric. Secure a double sewing thread at the marked position.

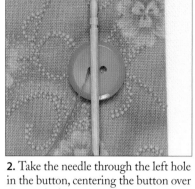

2. Take the needle through the left hole in the button, centering the button over the marked point. Place a spacer, over the button between the holes.

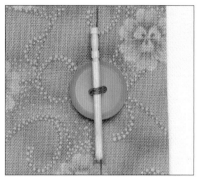

3. Stitch the button in place with several stitches over the spacer, working through the same holes in the fabric. Finish with the thread on the back.

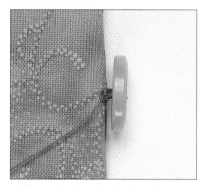

4. Bring the thread to the front between the fabric and the button. Remove the spacer.

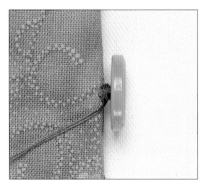

5. Wrap the thread around the stitching five or six times to create the shank.

6. Take the needle to the back and secure the thread.

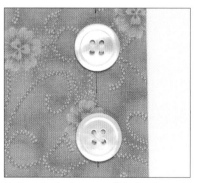

7. Four-hole button. Stitch through the holes in the same manner, working in straight pairs or in the form of an X.

hand stitching reinforced button

Stitching a small reinforcing button on the wrong side of the garment behind the main button provides strength at points of great strain. This small button takes the stress that would otherwise be on the fabric. Both buttons must have the same number of holes. If the fabric is delicate, or in an area that can't be interfaced, substitute a doubled square of fabric or reinforcing tape for the button.

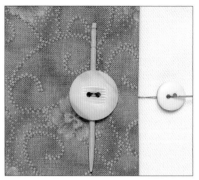

1. Begin to attach the main button using a spacer as described on page 55. Place a small button on the wrong side directly behind the main button.

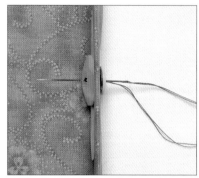

2. Stitch through the holes in both buttons. Finish by taking the needle and thread to the front and complete the shank. Secure the thread by stitching through the shank several times.

hand stitching shank buttons

Mark the position for the button on the fabric and secure the doubled thread at this point. Place the button over the marked point with the shank parallel to the buttonhole position. Stitch the button in place, taking the needle through the fabric close to the base of the shank.

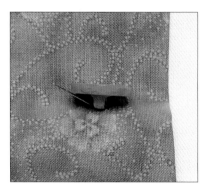

hints shank buttons

If the shank on the chosen button isn't high enough for the fabric thickness, add a little height by working a thread shank when attaching the buttons.

Avoid using buttons with a high shank on the back of garments intended for babies or toddlers because the shank will press into the child's back when he or she is lying down.

casings

A casing is a tunnel formed on a garment to enclose elastic or a drawstring. All casings should be slightly wider than the elastic or the drawstring to allow for free movement. Folded casings are made using an allowance given on the pattern and applied casings are formed using a separate piece of fabric. A folded casing is usually restricted to straight edges, but can cope with a gentle curve if the casing isn't too wide.

A facing can be attached to make an applied casing which works well for casings on curves because the facing can be made from fabric cut on the bias or from purchased bias binding. Non-roll elastic is used for waistbands to ensure the casing stays flat.

Cut a length of elastic slightly less than the circumference of the body where the casing sits, such as the waist or wrist, plus ¾" for an overlap to join the ends.

folded casing with elastic

1. Finish the raw edge with a zigzag or overlock stitch, or press under ¼". Fold the casing to the wrong side for the required depth and pin.

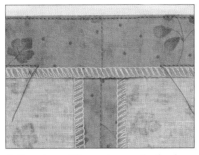

2. Leaving a 3" opening at the back or side seam, stitch along the finished edge to secure the casing. Topstitch along the folded edge to hold the elastic firmly in the casing.

3. Attach a safety pin to one end of the elastic. Secure the other end to the fabric near the opening to stop it from slipping into the casing. Work the elastic through the casing using the safety pin.

4. Ensuring that the elastic isn't twisted within the casing, overlap the ends and pin. Stitch a square with a cross in the middle on the overlap or work zigzag stitching to secure the ends.

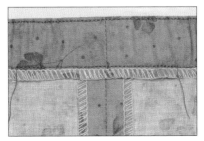

5. Pull the ends of the elastic into the casing. Reposition the edges of the opening and stitch closed.

folded casing with ruffle

By folding a deeper amount of fabric than is needed for inserting elastic or a drawstring, you can create a ruffle at the top of the facing. The sewing is done flat, but when the elastic or string is inserted to gather the waistband or cuff, a ruffle forms.

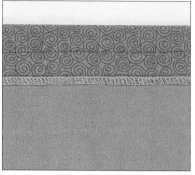

1. Leaving the ends open or an opening at a seam, fold and stitch the lower edge of the casing as before. Work another line of stitching above the first to create the casing.

2. Thread elastic through the casing and finish as required. The upper section of the casing forms the ruffle.

drawstring casing

Stitch two vertical buttonholes in the center of the casing before it is folded and stitched. Make the casing as described on page 57, but without leaving an opening. Insert the drawstring through the buttonholes.

partial casing

Partial casings can be used at the back or sides of garments. Fold and stitch the casing following the instructions for folded casing, leaving the ends open. Insert the elastic into the casing, securing the ends with stitching just inside the seam allowance.

hints casings

After inserting the drawstring and making sure the ends that extend out of the casing are even, you can machine stitch through the casing at the back of the garment along the seam line to ensure that the drawstring stays in place and doesn't accidentally come out during laundering.

You can combine the snug fit of elastic with the look of drawstrings. Cut a piece of elastic that is about half of the waist measurement, and then attach a drawstring end to each end of the elastic. Weave through the casing as usual and tie the strings. The gathers will be more uniform in the back and require less adjusting than with a full drawstring.

applied casings

An applied casing is a strip of fabric attached to a flat area where there is no seam to form a casing. It may be stitched onto the right or wrong side of the garment. A separate piece of fabric can also be applied on the upper edge of pants and skirts or the lower edge of a sleeve as shown on page 135. This is called a "faced casing" and is useful to reduce bulk when using a heavyweight fabric.

Preparation

Cut a piece of fabric the same width as the elastic or band plus ⅝" to allow for a ¼" seam allowance on each long edge as well as ease. The length of the fabric strip is determined by the length at the point where the casing is applied, plus a seam allowance at each end.

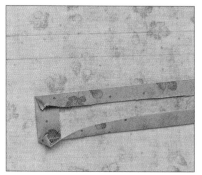

1. Continuous casing. Press under the seam allowance at each end of the strip, and then along the upper and lower edges. Mark the casing center line on the garment. Mark a second line, half the width of the finished casing, above the first.

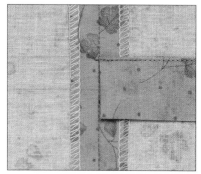

2. Pin and stitch the casing strip to the garment, aligning the upper edge with the upper line. When you return to the starting point, butt the two ends of the casing together.

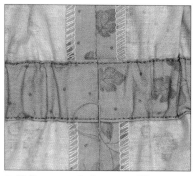

3. Follow steps 3–5 on page 57 to insert the elastic. Hand stitch the opening closed.

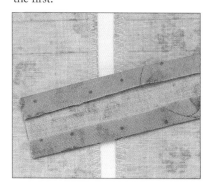

1. Open casing. Press under the seam allowance of the fabric strip on the upper and lower edges only. Mark the center and upper placement lines of the casing as in step 1.

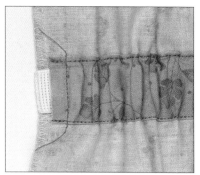

2. Pin and stitch the casing in place. Pin one end of the elastic near one end of the casing. Insert the elastic through the casing and machine baste the end just inside the seam allowance to secure.

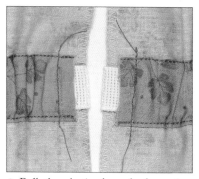

3. Pull the elastic through the casing and secure the remaining end as before.

clipping and notching

After stitching a seam on a curved edge, the seam allowance must be clipped to allow it to lie flat once the garment is turned to the right side. Use small, sharp, pointed scissors and take care to finish the cut within a few fabric threads of the stitching. If the clip is too close, the seam may fray at this point.

See also "Convex to Concave Curve" when one is stitched to the other on page 74, and "Clipping Corners" on page 126.

concave curves
clipping

Concave or inward-facing curves such as necklines or faced armholes need to be able to spread open when turned to lie in the opposite direction.

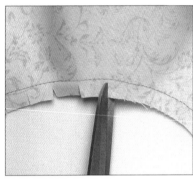

1. Clip a straight cut into the seam allowances at a right angle to the stitching.

2. When the seam is turned to the right side, the seam allowance spreads at the cut to lie flat.

convex curves
notching

Convex or outward facing curves such as the outer edge of a round collar, will compress when turned to the inside.

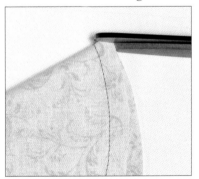

1. Fold the stitched curve at a right angle to the stitching and cut the seam allowance diagonally toward the stitching.

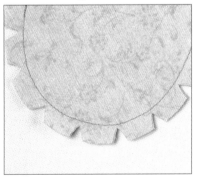

2. A small triangular notch is cut into the seam allowances. The tighter the curve, the wider and closer the notches should be.

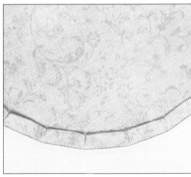

3. When the seam allowances are pressed to the wrong side, the notch closes up, allowing the seam allowances to lie flat.

scallops

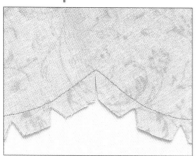

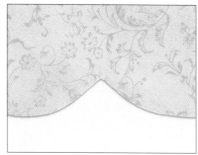

1. At the peak of a scallop, clip toward the peak, ending close to the stitching. Notch the curved areas.

2. When turned to the right side, the clip opens out, allowing the seam allowances to lie flat on the inside.

partial seams

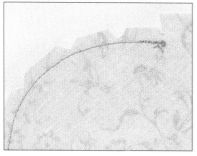

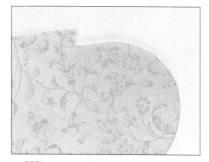

1. If a seam ends at a marked point and the remainder of the seam allowance is required for a further step, clip to the marked point close to the stitching.

2. When turned to the right side, the seam allowance remains intact, extending beyond the finished edge.

hems

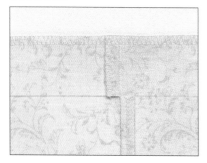

1. To reduce bulk in a hem or facing, clip the seam allowances at the fold. Press the seam allowances within the hem in the opposite direction from the main seam.

2. Fold the hem on the foldline. The seam allowances lie flat inside the hem. This method is not recommended for sheer fabrics.

hints **clipping**

Clip or notch a seam before trimming any excess, except when the seam requires grading. In that instance, grade first; then clip or notch.

When clipping any curve, the distance between the clips will depend on the tightness of the curve. The tighter the curve, the closer the clips or notches should be.

collars

Collars are often the most noticeable style element on a garment and are designed in many forms. They fall into three main groups: stand, flat, and rolled. The main factor in determining which group a collar falls into is the relationship between the neckline curve on the garment to that on the collar.

The styling of collars doesn't affect their basic construction because they commonly consist of two parts, the upper and under collar, or the collar and collar facing.

An important element to any collar is the interfacing used to define and support the shape. It is vital to balance the weight of the interfacing with the weight of the collar fabric. Interfacing is generally applied to the wrong side of the under collar, but as with any rule, there can be exceptions. Adding interfacing to the upper collar can provide stability for embroidery or other forms of embellishment. When constructing a collar from a very lightweight or pale fabric, consider applying interfacing to the wrong side of the upper collar to prevent the seam allowances from showing through on the right side.

flat collar

The neckline curve of a flat collar is very similar to the neckline edge of the garment, causing the collar to roll slightly and fall flat across the shoulder. The two collar pieces should be an exact mirror image of each other to achieve a balanced result. If the garment has a front opening, a flat collar is usually constructed in one piece that meets at the center front.

For a back-opening garment, the collar may have two pieces with the ends meeting at the center front and center back.

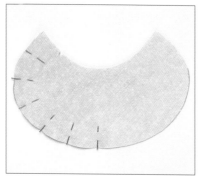

1. Apply interfacing to the wrong side of the under collar. Matching raw edges, pin the upper and under collar pieces right sides together.

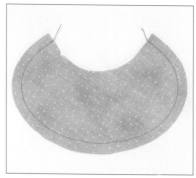

2. Stitch the collar seam, leaving the neck edge open.

3. Trim the seam allowances and grade if necessary. Notch the curves.

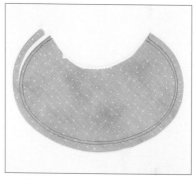

3a. Alternatively, stitch again ¹⁄₈" away from the first sewing line, within the seam allowance. Trim close to the second line of stitching.

4. Turn the collar to the right side. Roll the seam slightly toward the under collar and press lightly. Baste the raw edges together at the neckline.

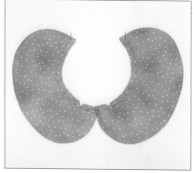

Two-piece collar. Construct the second half of the collar in the same manner. Secure the two pieces where they meet on the neckline, tacking them just inside the stitching line.

rolled collar

The neckline curve on the collar is often flat or slightly curved in the opposite direction to the garment. When attached, the collar stands high at the center back (the stand); then rolls to fall toward the shoulders (the fall). The fold between the stand and the fall is the roll line.

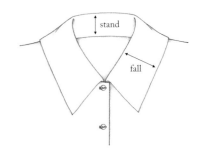

one-piece rolled collar

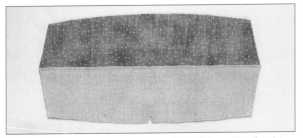

1. Apply interfacing to the wrong side of the collar, finishing at, or ⅛" past, the foldline. The interfaced section will be the under collar.

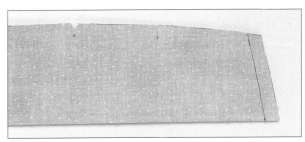

2. Fold the collar right sides together, matching raw edges. Stitch across the ends.

3. Trim the seam allowances and clip the corners.

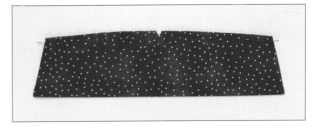

4. Turn the collar to the right side. Push out the corners and roll the seams slightly toward the under collar. Pin and baste the raw edges together at the neckline. Press lightly.

two-piece rolled collar

A rolled collar with a shaped edge will need to be constructed from two separate pieces.

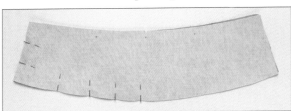

1. Apply interfacing to the wrong side of the under collar. Pin the upper and under collar right sides together.

hint corners

To define a corner, take a knotted thread through the collar and out at the corner. Pull on the thread to ease the corner out.

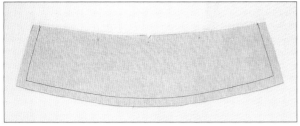

2. Stitch around the collar, pivoting at the corners. Leave the neck edges open.

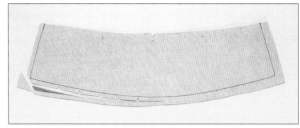

3. Trim the seam allowances and grade if necessary. Clip the corners and notch the curve.

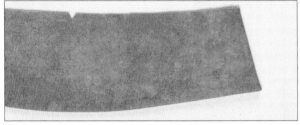

4. Turn the collar to the right side, rolling the seam slightly toward the underside. Push out the corners carefully. Press lightly.

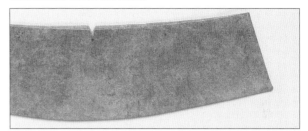

5. Baste the raw edges together at the neckline. Rolling the lower seam under may make a small difference in the position of the raw edges at the upper edge.

stand collar

Simple stand collars rise up from the neckline. Mandarin or Nehru collars are both examples of stand collars.

basic stand collar

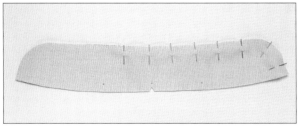

1. Apply interfacing to the wrong side of the under collar. Pin the upper and under collar pieces right sides together.

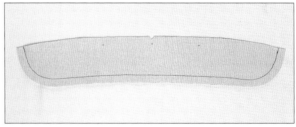

2. Stitch around the outer edge of the collar, leaving the neck edge open.

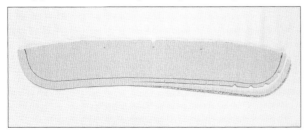

3. Trim the seam allowances and grade if necessary. Clip or notch the curves.

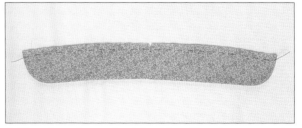

4. Turn the collar to the right side, rolling the seam to the edge. Baste the raw edges together at the neckline. Press lightly.

shirt collar

The shirt collar has two parts, the stand and the collar. The two sections are usually separate pieces but they can be designed as one.

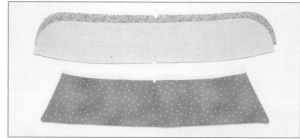

1. Construct a two-piece rolled collar following the steps on pages 64–65. Apply interfacing to the wrong side of one stand piece.

2. Matching centers, edges, and markings, pin the collar with the interfaced layer facing the uninterfaced stand piece.

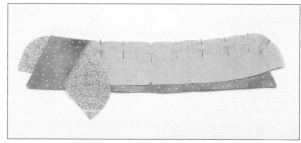

3. Baste the collar in place. Matching raw edges and centers, place the interfaced stand piece over the collar and pin.

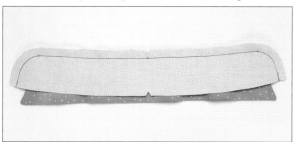

4. Stitch. Trim the seam allowances. Clip and notch the curves of the stand.

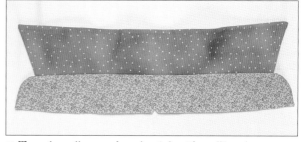

5. Turn the collar stand to the right side, rolling the seam to the edge on the ends of the stand. Press the collar away from the seam. Matching centers, baste the raw edges together.

shawl collar

A shawl collar is a variation of a rolled collar. A shawl collar can be narrow or quite wide and can be used on shirts, jackets, coats, and bathrobes, giving a soft unbroken line between the collar and the lapels. A shawl collar is often used in conjunction with a wrapped front opening, which has a soft tie belt to hold the fronts together, rather than a traditional button closure.

Preparation

Apply interfacing to the wrong side of the combined collar and front facing piece, omitting the hem area at the lower edges. Stay stitch around the corners between the collar and the shoulder seam. Clip diagonally into the corner on both pieces.

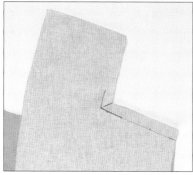

1. Garment shoulder seams. Pin and stitch the front pieces to the back, ending securely where the stitching lines meet at the neckline. Finish both of the seam allowances separately and press open.

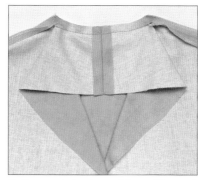

2. Garment back neckline. Pin and stitch the center back collar seam. Press the seam allowances open. Matching the seam with the center back, pin and stitch across the back neckline. Clip the curve.

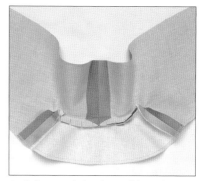

3. Collar and back neckline facing. Stitch the shoulder seams following step 1. Complete the collar and facing following step 2. Finish the outer edge of the facing.

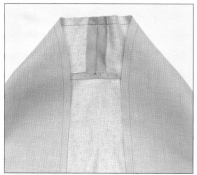

4. Attach the collar and front facing. With right sides together, matching centers and markings, pin the collar piece to the garment. Stitch in place, stitching each side from the center back to the hem.

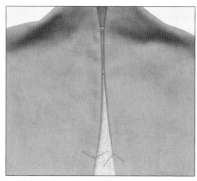

5. Trim the seam allowances and clip the curves. Turn to the right side and finger-press the seam. Referring to the pattern, mark the point on both sides of the front where the collar will begin to roll.

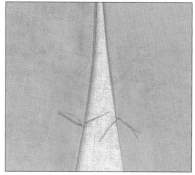

6. Press the front opening edges lightly, rolling the collar seam toward the garment between the marks and placing it on the edge below the marks.

7. Baste through all layers along the roll line and close to the outer edge.

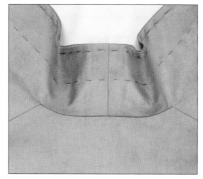

8. Matching shoulder seams and back neckline, pin the layers together. Stitch in the ditch from shoulder to shoulder across the back.

9. Hand stitch the edge of the facing to the shoulder seams. Finish the lower edge of the facings following the instructions on page 93.

attaching collars

There are three main ways to attach a collar to a neckline—using a continuous facing or lining, using a facing on both sides of the opening edge only, or applying the collar directly to the neckline. While the instructions show a different collar for each method, the method isn't limited to the collar style depicted.

continuous facing or lining

Preparation

Construct your chosen collar. Stay stitch the neckline on the garment pieces. Apply interfacing to the wrong side of the back and front facings. Stitch and finish the shoulder seams of the garment and the facings. Finish the outer edge of the facing.

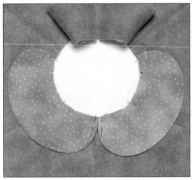

1. Matching raw edges, centers, and shoulder marks, pin the collar to the neckline.

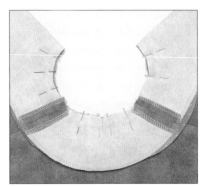

2. Baste the collar in place. Matching raw edges, centers, and seams, pin the facing over the neckline, sandwiching the collar in between.

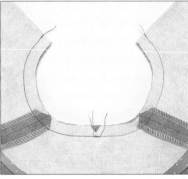

3. Beginning at the center back, stitch the neckline seam through all layers. Return to the center back and stitch the remainder of the seam.

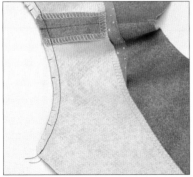

4. Trim and grade the seam allowances if necessary. Clip the curve and trim the corners.

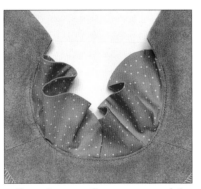

5. Press the seam allowances toward the facing. Understitch close to the seam line on the facing.

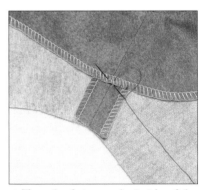

6. Turn the facing to the inside of the garment. Matching seams, hand stitch the facing to the garment shoulder seams.

front facings only

Preparation

Construct your chosen collar. Stay stitch the neckline on the garment pieces. Apply interfacing to the wrong side of the front facings. Stitch and finish the shoulder seams in the garment. Finish the outer edge of the facings. Press under the seam allowances on the shoulder edges of the facings. Cut a length of 2"-wide bias binding. The length of the binding is determined by the measurement across the back neck plus ¾" at each end. Fold the binding in half along the length and press.

1. Bias-binding method: Matching raw edges and center front and back marks, pin and tack the collar to the neckline.

2. Matching raw edges and the folded edge on each facing to the garment shoulder seams, pin the front facings to the neckline. The ends of the collar are sandwiched in between. Baste the facings and collar in place.

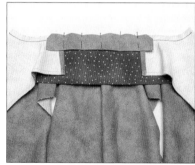

3. Matching raw edges, pin the binding across the back neck and over the ends of the facings. Stitch through all layers. Trim the seam allowances and clip the curve and corners.

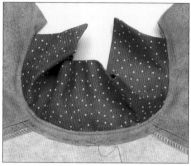

4. Turn the binding and facings to the right side and understitch on the facing and binding. Hand stitch the binding to the neckline and the facing to the shoulder seams.

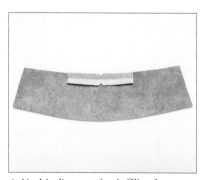

1. No-binding method: Clip the seam allowances to the marked shoulder points on the upper collar. Baste the raw edges together on the front sections of the collar, folding the clipped seam allowances back.

2. With right sides together, pin the under collar in place, matching seams and marks. Baste the collar to the neckline from the ends to the clipped points. Baste only the under collar across the back neckline.

3. Pin the front facings over the neckline, sandwiching the ends of the collar. Keeping the upper collar seam allowances folded back between the clips, stitch around the neckline.

4. Trim the seam allowances and clip the curve and corners. Clip the seam allowances level with the ends of the facings. Turn the facings to the right side.

5. Trim the folded seam allowances on the upper collar. Press the back neckline seam allowances toward the collar. Align the fold with the previous stitching line. Pin and hand stitch. Secure the facings.

attaching a stand collar

Preparation. Construct your chosen collar. Leave the raw edges free at the neckline. Stay stitch the neckline on the garment pieces. Stitch and finish the shoulder seams. Finish the front opening edges with facings or button bands.

1. Clip the neckline at approximately ¾" intervals. This will allow the collar to fit smoothly onto the neckline.

2. With right sides together and matching raw edges and markings, pin and then baste the raw edge of the interfaced stand to the neckline.

3. Stitch the seam, securing the ends. Trim the seam allowance, grading it if necessary.

4. Press the seam allowances toward the stand. Press under the seam allowances on the remaining raw edge and trim to ¼". Matching the marks, align the folded edge with the previous stitching line, pin, and hand stitch.

5. Press. On the right side of the stand, topstitch close to the edge if desired.

Corners

Producing a beautifully finished corner is a combination of careful stitching, clipping, turning, and pressing. The method used will depend on the weight of the fabric and the angle of the corner. When finishing edges such as hems and bindings, the corners are best formed using mitering techniques: folded, stitched, or a combination of both.

stitching a corner seam

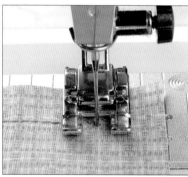

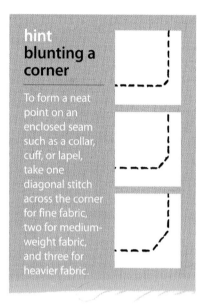

1. Stitch the seam toward the corner. Stop with the needle down at the corner point. The distance to the front edge of the fabric should equal the seam-allowance width.

2. With the needle in the fabric, lift the presser foot. Pivot the fabric until the adjacent raw edge is aligned with the seam guide. Lower the presser foot and continue.

hint
blunting a corner

To form a neat point on an enclosed seam such as a collar, cuff, or lapel, take one diagonal stitch across the corner for fine fabric, two for medium-weight fabric, and three for heavier fabric.

attaching inner to outer corners

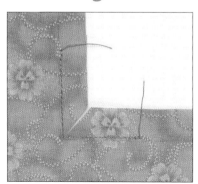

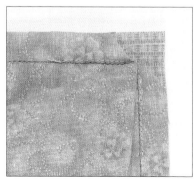

1. Stay stitch the inner corner just inside the seam allowance. Clip to the point, taking care not to cut the stitching.

2. Spread the clipped section to fit the outer corner. Match raw edges and pin. With the clipped fabric on top, stitch the seam, pivoting at the corner.

3. Press the seam allowances toward the clipped fabric.

box corner

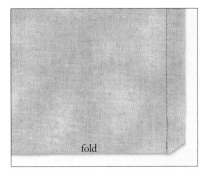

1. Fold the fabric, right sides together, and stitch the side seam. Clip the corner almost to the stitching.

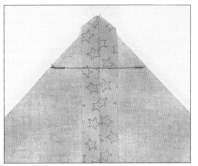

2. Press the seam allowances open. Refold the fabric, matching the seam to the previous fold line. At the required measurement, pin and stitch at a right angle to the previous seam.

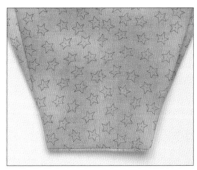

3. Trim away the excess fabric at the point if necessary and finish the seam. Turn to the right side. Repeat on the opposite corner.

finishing corners
mitered
turned hem

This mitered corner makes a neat finish when hemming a right-angled corner. It might be used to secure the hem and front opening of an unlined jacket, the corner of a hem, or the side vent of a shirt. For quilts, blankets, and place mats, you can use this method to attach a lining while finishing the outer edge at the same time. The hem must be the same depth on both sides of the corner.

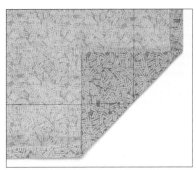

1. Finish the raw edges, and then press under the required hem allowance on both sides and unfold. Fold the corner diagonally, aligning the previous fold lines. Press.

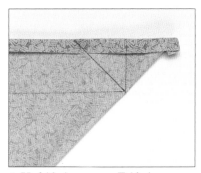

2. Unfold the corner. Fold the corner diagonally, right sides together and matching finished edges. Stitch along the previous diagonal crease.

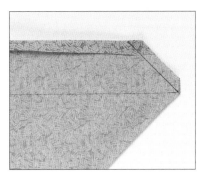

3. Trim the corner, leaving a ¼" seam allowance. Clip the point.

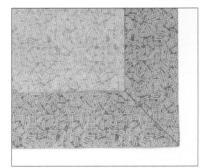

4. Press the seam allowances open. Turn to the right side. Hand stitch the hems in place or topstitch on the right side, pivoting at the corner.

mitered binding

These instructions apply to both single and double binding. The following steps are worked using a double binding.

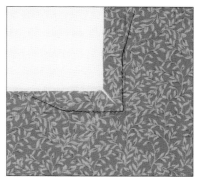

1. Inner corner. Stay stitch the corner just inside the seam allowance. Clip into the corner almost up to the stitching.

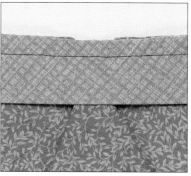

2. Press the binding in half lengthwise. Spread the cut corner and with right sides together, pin the binding to the edge. Stitch along the seam line.

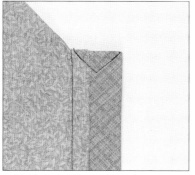

3. Fold the binding right sides together at the corner. Stitch from the seam to the outer corner in a V, slightly more shallow than the width of the binding.

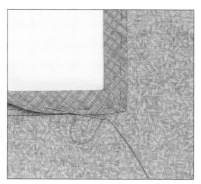

4. Trim the seam allowances and clip into the point. Fold the binding over the seam allowances. Pin, and then hand stitch the binding in place along the previous sewing line.

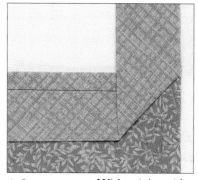

1. Outer corner. With right sides together, pin and stitch the binding along the seam line, ending securely at the seam-turning point. Fold the binding diagonally from the corner, covering the previous stitching. Press the diagonal fold.

2. Refold the binding, matching raw edges on the second edge. The upper fold should be at a right angle to the point. Stitch along the second edge, starting at the corner point.

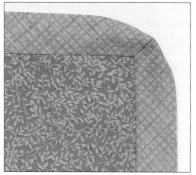

3. Press the binding away from the fabric. Fold the binding over the seam allowances to the wrong side, forming a miter at the corner on the right side.

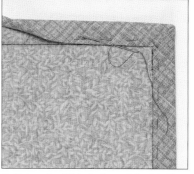

4. Bring the folded edge of the binding to match the previous stitching line, forming a miter at the corner on the wrong side. Pin, and then hand stitch in place along the previous stitching line.

similar curves

When joining similar curves, such as the crotch of a pair of pants, a section of the seam may be on the bias. Because the seam may be strained during wear, stitches can break unless care is taken when stitching the seam. The longer the stitches, the more likely they are to break.

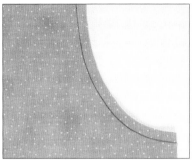

1. With right sides together, pin and stitch the two pieces using a short machine stitch. Stitch the tightest part of the curve again.

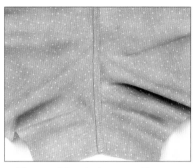

2. Trim and finish the seam allowances. Press the seam allowances to one side.

convex to concave curve

Stitching two pieces together with dissimilar curves, such as a princess seam running over the bust, requires careful marking, pinning, and clipping to ensure that the seam follows the contours of the body. Refer to page 60 for clipping and notching.

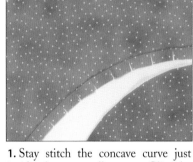

1. Stay stitch the concave curve just inside the seam allowance. Clip the tightest part of the curve.

2. With right sides facing, match the markings and pin the two pieces together. Spread the clipped edge slightly to fit the curve. Baste. Stitch the seam with the clipped side on top.

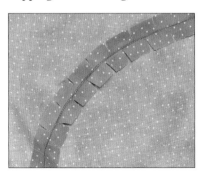

3. Trim the seam allowances and finger-press open. Notch the fullness on the convex curve, offsetting the clips and notches wherever possible.

4. Press flat with the point of the iron. Take care not to press into the garment, thereby creating creases.

5. Press the seam allowances open over a curved surface such as a tailor's ham.

hints
curves

When stitching a straight edge to a curved edge, the seam allowances along the straight edge must be clipped to allow it to fit the curved edge of the other pattern piece.

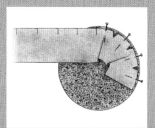

When stitching a curve, guide the fabric through the machine slowly, keeping the raw edges aligned with the seam guide.

darts

Darts are used to shape flat fabric, enabling a garment to follow the curves of the body. They occur mostly on women's clothing to contour the bust, waist, and hips. The pattern will indicate in which direction to press the dart. Hori-zontal darts are pressed downward and vertical darts are most commonly pressed toward the center.

basic dart

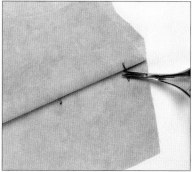

1. Mark the darts with tailor's tacks following the instructions on page 26.

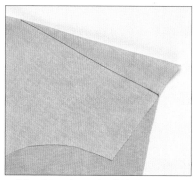

2. Matching the tacks, fold the dart and pin. Stitch the dart from the outer edge toward the point. Secure the stitching at the point by backstitching for approximately ³⁄₈".

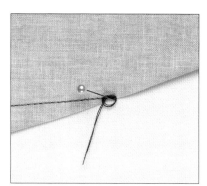

2a. Alternatively, tie the thread tails together. Tighten the knot, adjusting it with a pin to settle on the fabric.

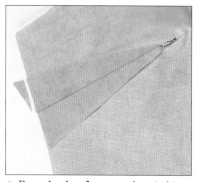

3. Press the dart flat to set the stitching. Then press the dart to one side as indicated on the pattern, or for thicker fabrics, cut the dart open to within ⁵⁄₈" of the point. Trim the sides of the dart and press open.

contour dart

A contour dart is often long and shapes the fabric at the waist of a garment. It has a point at each end and the widest part at the center.

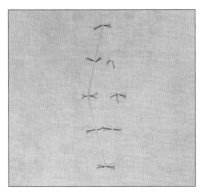

1. Transfer all the pattern markings for the dart with tailor's tacks following the instructions on page 26.

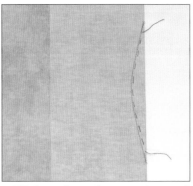

2. With right sides together and matching marks, fold the dart along the center. Pin and baste. Stitch the dart, securing as described on page 75.

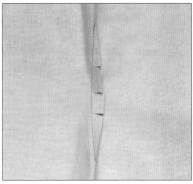

3. Remove the basting. Clip the dart to 1/8" from the stitching so the fold lies flat. Press the dart to one side.

french dart

A French dart appears on the front of a garment extending from the hip or waist side seam to the bust. This type of dart is wider than a basic dart and is curved. Therefore it must be cut to open the center before stitching. If curved, the upper line is shorter than the lower and the two must be eased to fit.

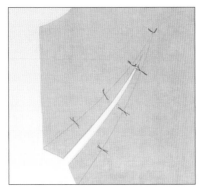

1. Transfer the pattern markings including the center cut line. Remove the pattern and cut the dart.

2. With right sides together and matching stitching lines and marks, pin and baste. Stitch the dart starting at the outer edge, securing at the point.

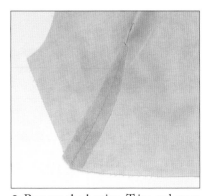

3. Remove the basting. Trim and press the dart open.

darts

easing

Easing is necessary when attaching two edges of differing lengths, such as fitting the shoulder cap of a sleeve into the armhole. The longer edge is eased to fit the shorter one. Small amounts of ease can be accommodated with careful pinning, but areas of greater ease will require a row of machine stitching just inside the seam allowance to control fullness.

Preparation

Stitch a row of machine basting just inside the seam line of the longer piece. Mark the center of the area to be eased on the edge of both fabric pieces. For a small amount of ease, you may omit the machine basting.

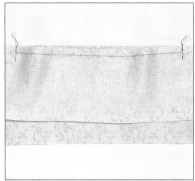

1. Matching pattern markings and raw edges, pin the fabrics together at each end of the section, placing the pins at a right angle to the edge.

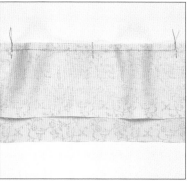

2. Pin to match the centers. Ensure there is an even amount of loose fabric on both sides of the center pin.

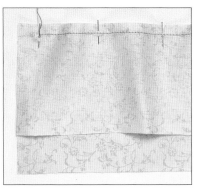

3. Distributing the fabric evenly, place the next pin midway between the center and outer pins. Repeat on the other side. Continue in this manner until the pins are close together.

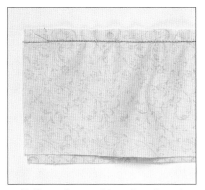

4. Pull up the machine thread, easing the fullness to fit. Ensure there are no obvious pleats. Baste the fabrics together and check to make sure there are no pleats. Adjust as necessary, and then stitch.

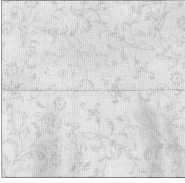

5. Trim and finish the seam. Press carefully to steam out any rippling that may be visible on the eased side of the seam.

elastic

The following instructions are for simple techniques to attach elastic without a fabric casing. See also "Casings" on page 57.

quick thread casing for narrow elastic

A thread casing is an easy, attractive method to create an elasticized edge for a variety of garments. It is best worked on light- to mediumweight fabrics only. Use strong polyester thread to increase the durability of the casing.

Preparation

Cut a length of elastic to fit comfortably around the body at the required position, plus seam allowances. Stitch and finish any seams, leaving one seam open. Finish the raw edge below the casing using the desired method. It is easier to do this while the fabric is still flat.

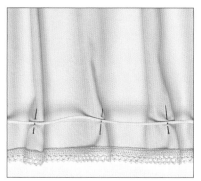

1. Mark a line on the wrong side of the fabric at the position for the elastic. Divide the line and the elastic into quarters and mark. Matching marks, pin the elastic to the fabric. Secure the ends of the elastic with stitching within the seam allowance.

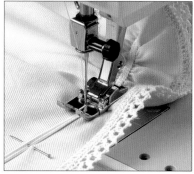

2. Using a zigzag stitch fractionally wider than the elastic, stitch over the elastic without catching it. Stretch the elastic to fit flat against the fabric between the pinned positions as you stitch. Holding the fabric flat behind the presser foot is helpful.

3. Stitch the final seam to secure the ends of the elastic. Make sure that the ends of the elastic match, keeping the trimming aligned at the lower edge.

hints elastic

Almost all forms of elastic will eventually lose their stretch. The time frame will depend on the amount of wear and the care taken when laundering. Choose a method that allows the elastic to ride freely inside a casing if you expect to replace it.

Constant exposure to chlorine or salt water will shorten the life of general-purpose elastic. Special swimwear elastic, which is resistant to the damage caused by these elements, has been developed for this purpose.

attaching underwear elastic

Use the one-step technique when attaching narrow, decorative elastic to the edges of underwear. The two-step method is best used when applying wide elastic as a waistband.

Preparation

For both methods, cut a length of elastic to fit comfortably around the body at the required position, plus seam allowances. Stitch and finish any seams passing through the position for the elastic, leaving one seam open. Finish the raw edge with a zigzag or overlock stitch. Divide the garment edge and the length of elastic into quarters and mark. Matching marks and with the right side of the elastic facing up, pin the marked edge of the elastic to the right side of the fabric. Position the elastic to overlap the fabric by ¼".

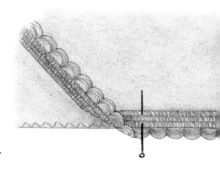

one-step method

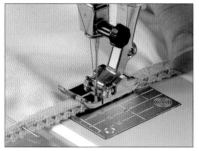

1. Using a wide, open zigzag or a tricot stitch at the widest setting, stitch along the heading of the elastic, stretching it to fit flat against the fabric between the pins.

2. Stitch the final seam to secure the elastic ends.

two-step method

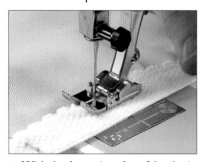

1. With the decorative edge of the elastic toward the garment, pin the upper edge to overlap the fabric by ¼". Using a medium-width zigzag, stitch along the edge of the elastic. Stretch and flatten as you stitch.

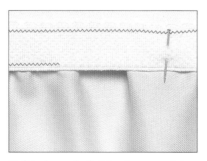

2. Stitch and finish the remaining garment side seam. Fold the elastic to the wrong side. Pin the lower edge to the fabric at the marked divisions. Stretch the elastic flat as you stitch.

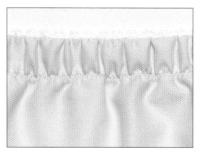

3. On the right side, the upper edge of the elastic forms a decorative finish.

elastic

facings

A facing is used to finish the raw edges and give stability to particular areas of a garment. There are two basic types of facings, separate and integrated. A separate facing is cut using a pattern piece the same shape and on the same grain as the edge it will finish. An integrated facing is an extension of the garment piece. After a facing is attached, it is turned to the wrong side and secured. It should not show on the right side. If the garment is being made from heavyweight fabric, a lighter fabric can be used for facings to reduce bulk. See also: "Faced Armhole" on page 34, "Faced Necklines" on page 101, "Faced or False Hem" on page 93, and "Faced Waistline" on page 145.

Preparation

Stay stitch the neckline and armhole edges of the front and back bodice pieces. Apply lightweight interfacing to the wrong side of the facing pieces. Mark the end of the seam line on the bodice pieces at both ends of the shoulder seam. For bias facing, cut the bias facing twice the desired finished width, adding seam allowances. The length should equal the distance of the seam line between the opening fold lines (shown opposite). Finish the raw edges of the opening and press the fold lines.

combination facing

On a sleeveless garment with narrow shoulders, it is preferable to cut the armhole and neckline facings as a combined piece. If cut separately, they create bulk at the shoulder seams.

1. Pin and stitch the bodice front to the back at the sides. Finish the seam allowances separately and press open.

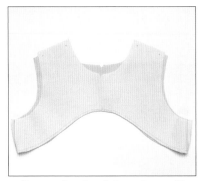

2. Repeat for the facing pieces. Also finish the lower edge of the facing.

3. With right sides together, pin the facing to the bodice around the armholes and neckline. Offset the garment edges by ⅟₁₆" at the shoulder point. Stitch each seam to the marked point.

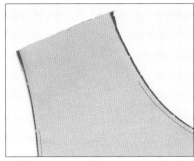

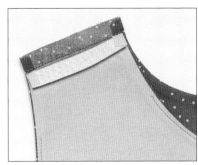

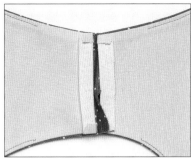

4. Trim seam allowances and clip curves. Turn right side out. Understitch the seams on the facing, beginning and ending as far as you can reach toward the shoulders. At the shoulders, the facing will roll slightly to the inside. Press.

5. With right sides together and keeping the facing seam allowances out of the way, stitch the bodice front to the back at the shoulders.

6. Trim the seam allowances and finger-press open. Push the shoulder seams through the opening and toward the back of the garment, keeping them flat.

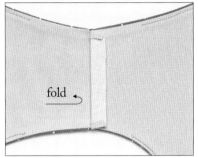

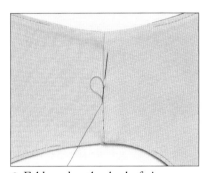

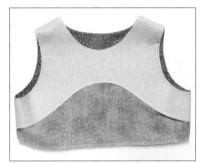

7. Trim the facing seam allowances. Fold the front facing seam allowance to the inside through the opening.

8. Fold under the back facing seam allowances, and hand stitch the opening closed.

9. Press. Aligning the seams, hand stitch the facing to the bodice at the underarm seam.

bias facing

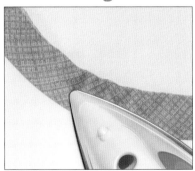

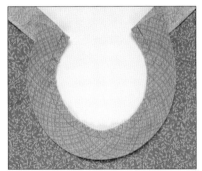

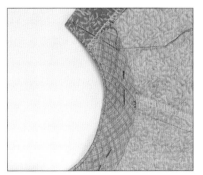

1. Fold the bias facing in half lengthwise. Using a steam iron, shape the folded facing, stretching the folded edge to fit the neckline curve, keeping the raw edges even.

2. Fold the opening facings right sides together and pin. With right sides together and matching raw edges, pin, baste and stitch the bias facing to the neckline.

3. Trim the seam allowances and corners. Turn the facings to the inside and push out the corners. Understitch the neckline on the bias facing. Hand stitch the binding to the shoulder seams and the facing to the binding.

fasteners

A fastener secures an opening that allows a garment to be taken on and off easily. Buttons, zippers, hooks and eyes, and snaps are all simple or decorative types of fasteners or closures. See also "Buttonholes" on pages 45–49, "Buttons" on pages 54–56, and "Zippers" on pages 146–150.

hook and eye

This fastener should be used on opening edges that butt together.

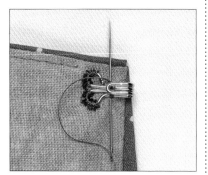

1. Position the hook on the inside of one edge. Whipstich around each hole. Bring the thread to the front near the shaft. Whipstich over the shaft to hold the hook flat against the fabric.

2. Position the eye in the corresponding position on the opposite edge. Whip-stitch around each hole then stitch over the arms of the eye to hold the eye flat against the fabric.

hook and bar

This fastening type is used for added strength on waistbands.

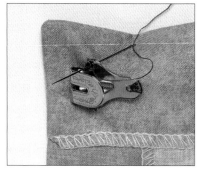

1. Sew the hook into position on the wrong side of the overlap, ensuring that the stitching doesn't show on the right side.

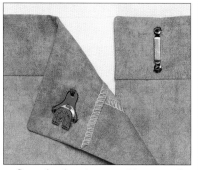

2. Sew the bar into position on the opposite edge of the opening to correspond to the hook placement.

hook and thread loop

An alternative to the metal eye is a blanket-stitched loop or bar.

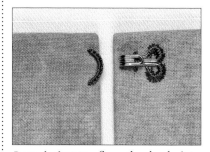

Butted closure. Sew the hook into position on one edge of the opening. Mark the upper and lower placement of thread loop to correspond on the other edge of the opening. Stitch the loop following the instructions on page 53.

Lapped closure. Stitch the hook as before on the wrong side of the overlap. Mark and stitch the thread loop at the corresponding position on the underlap.

hook-and-loop tape

Hook-and-loop tape can be used as an alternative to traditional hook closures for over-lapped openings. Generally, the hooked nap tape is sewn to the underside of the overlap, allowing it to be pressed into the fuzzy nap to make the connection more secure.

With the two tapes pressed together, measure and cut the length needed to secure the opening. Pull the tapes apart and stitch the fuzzy tape into position on the underlap by stitching around the edge. Place the overlap in position on the tape and mark the placement of the hook tape. Stitch the hook tape in place in the same manner.

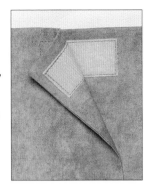

sew-on snaps

These small fasteners are used on closures with very little strain. They come in a range of sizes to suit the application. They are made from metal or clear plastic and consist of a ball section that fits into a socket section.

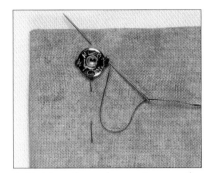

1. Position the socket section on the underlap ¼" from the upper edge. Stitch in place with overcast stitches into each hole.

2. Lap the closure and mark the position of the ball section on the overlap. Attach this section in a similar manner, carrying the thread between the layers of fabric.

Lingerie strap. Designed to hold bra straps in place, these can be purchased readymade or constructed using narrow ribbon and a snap. Stitch in place on the shoulder seam.

snap studs

A no-sew snap stud is a stronger grip version of the sew-on snap. It's useful for areas of greater strain, especially on denim, leather, and the inside leg openings of baby wear. A special assembly tool is required and is often supplied with the snap stud kit.

1. Position and attach the upper section of the stud on the wrong side of the overlap, following the manufacturer's instructions.

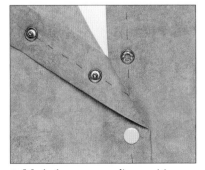

2. Mark the corresponding position on the underlap and repeat for the stud socket.

gathering

Gathering is a technique that draws in a greater amount of fabric to fit a smaller area. Gathers are most often used at waistlines, sleeve cuffs, below yokes, and for ruffles. For gentle gathering, the fabric allowance should be twice the finished width and for full gathers, three times the width or more, depending on the weight of the fabric. Gathers drape best on the straight grain. When gathering extended lengths, divide the area into smaller sections to make the gathering more manageable and to avoid broken threads. Leaving long thread tails, stop and start the gathering rows at each section. Refer to your machine manual for correct stitch length and tension for gathering.

attaching a gathered edge

Preparation

Gathering is usually done after all construction seams in the gathered fabric and the garment piece have been stitched, finished, and pressed. On some pieces, such as the head of a sleeve, the gathering rows are easier to stitch while the piece is flat.

To ensure the gathering is even, divide the edge of the gathering fabric and the edge of the garment into quarters. Mark the points on the edge of the fabric. When attaching a gathered skirt to the lower edge of a bodice, these marks will be the center front, center back, and the side seams.

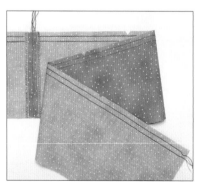 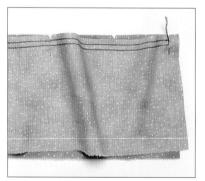 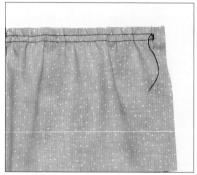

1. Stitching on the right side, work two rows of gathering (machine-basting) stitches ³⁄₁₆" from the seam line on either side.

2. With right sides together and matching marks, pin the gathered fabric to the garment edge. Anchor the bobbin threads at one end by winding around a pin in a figure-8 fashion.

3. Pull on the free bobbin thread tails while gliding the fabric along the threads into even gathers. When the first section fits the garment edge, tie the bobbin threads together to secure.

4. Release the bobbin threads at the other end and gather the next section in the same manner. Tie the thread tails together. Even out the gathers along the entire length and pin at regular intervals.

5. Readjust the machine stitch length and tension for normal sewing. Stitch the gathered fabric to the garment, placing the stitching halfway between the gathering rows.

6. Trim and finish the seam. Pull out the gathering threads. Press the seam allowances toward the flat fabric, using only the tip of the iron to avoid creasing the gathers.

joining two gathered edges

This type of seam is not very strong and the stitching may break under strain. It requires a "stay" to reinforce the seam, allowing it to retain its original shape. Stays can be created from any narrow strip with finished edges and a straight grain such as cotton twill tape, ribbon, or woven seam binding.

Preparation

Cut a piece of stay tape to match the finished length of the seam. Transfer any pattern markings to the tape. Stitch gathering rows on the edge of both pieces of fabric following step 1, opposite.

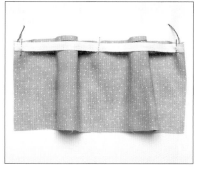

1. With the markings matching, center the tape along the seam line on the wrong side of the first fabric piece. Matching markings, pin to the fabric.

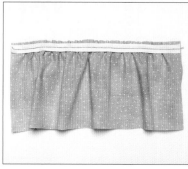

2. Gather the fabric to match the tape, Baste the tape in place along the center.

3. With right sides together and matching raw edges and markings, pin the ungathered edge of the second fabric piece to the first. Gather to fit the tape. Stitch along the previous stitching line. Trim and finish the seam.

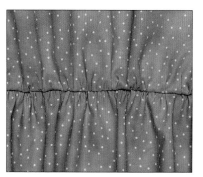

4. Open the joined pieces and finger-press the seam allowances upward. It should not require pressing with an iron.

hand stitching

The sewing machine can be the home sewer's best friend, but there are still many instances where neat hand stitching is required to give a superior finish to a garment.

Select a needle suitable for the thread and the particular stitch you are using. A fine needle with a small eye is best. Choose a short needle for single stitches like hemming and a longer needle for taking multiple stitches at one time such as the running stitch.

The thread should be strong and suited to the purpose and the fiber content of the fabric. Use matching thread for permanent stitching, so that it will be invisible. Using short lengths of good quality thread and trying not to twist the needle excessively will also help prevent knotting and twisting. When twisting does occur, let the needle hang freely on the thread, so that it can untwist.

knotting a thread

Use a knot to secure the beginning of temporary stitching because the basting thread can be removed easily by pulling on the knot.

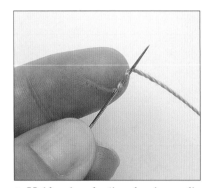

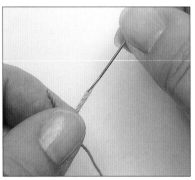

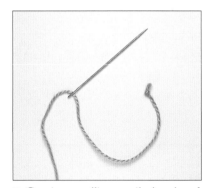

1. Hold a thread tail under the needle with your left index finger. Depending on the size of the knot, wrap the thread around the needle two or three times.

2. Hold the wraps firmly between your thumb and index finger. Slowly pull the threaded needle through.

3. Continue pulling until the thread resists. Tug the knot to lock it in position. Trim the tail close to the knot.

backstitch

Although the backstitch isn't usually used to construct a whole garment, it's still one of the most versatile of the hand stitches. Backstitching is useful to repair seams where it isn't practical to use a sewing machine. A few backstitches worked over each other is also the most efficient way to begin and end a line of hand stitching without using knots.

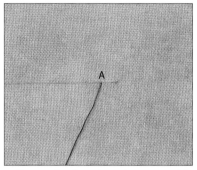

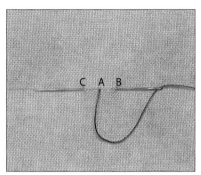

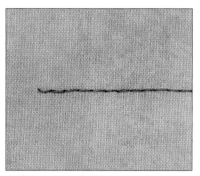

1. Secure the thread on the wrong side of the fabric. Bring the thread to the front at A, a short distance ahead of where the stitching should begin.

2. Insert the needle at B and bring it back up at C. The distance from C to A should be the same as the distance from A to B. Pull the thread through.

3. Continue stitching in the same manner. To end off, take the thread to the back through the last hole of the previous stitch. Notice that a row of backstitching looks similar to a row of machine stitching.

blanket stitch

Traditionally used in embroidery, this stitch can also be used to finish fabric edges or decoratively secure a narrow folded hem during garment construction. Another use is forming thread loops, as shown on pages 38 and 53. Work from left to right with the edge of the fabric and the tip of the needle toward you.

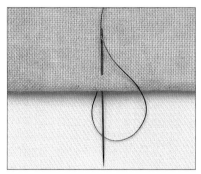

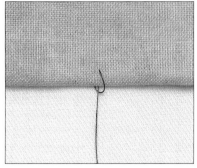

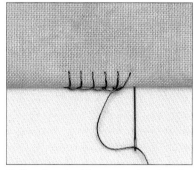

1. Secure the thread and bring it to the front below the edge of the fabric. With the thread under the tip, take the needle through the fabric and out under the fabric edge.

2. Pull the thread through and settle the loop on the fabric edge.

3. Continue in this manner, keeping the depth of the stitches even and at right angles to the fabric edge. To end, take the thread to the back and secure.

ladder stitch

When an opening is left in a seam to allow sections of a garment to be turned through to the right side, use the ladder stitch to close the opening with concealed stitching.

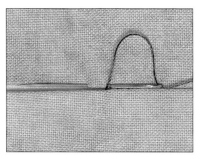 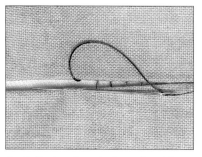 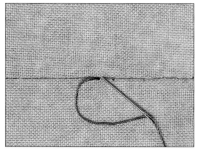

1. Secure the thread in the seam. Bring the needle to the front on the fold on one side of the opening. Beginning level with the emerging thread, take a small stitch through the fold on the opposite side of the opening.

2. Pull the thread through without closing the opening. Take a few more stitches in a similar manner, alternating back and forth between the edges of the opening.

3. Gently pull on the thread to bring the edges of the opening together. Con-tinue stitching from side to side, closing the opening after every few stitches. Secure the thread in the seam on the wrong side.

overcast or whip stitch

This stitch is used to finish a raw edge by hand. Fold over the fabric edges and then bring the needle through the fabric ⅛" from the edge. Pull the thread through. Take another stitch ¼" from the first. Continue stitching along the edge in the same manner.

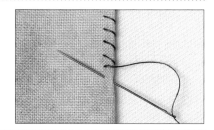

running stitch

This stitch can be both functional and decorative. The running stitch is made in a similar manner to basting, but the stitches are quite small and evenly spaced. Take the needle in and out of the fabric, picking up a number of stitches on the needle before pulling the thread through. The stitches should be approximately ⅛" long on both sides of the fabric.

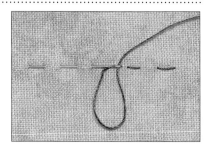

basting

Basting is useful to hold surfaces together in the correct position until you can machine stitch them. Avoid securing the ends because this will make it difficult to remove the thread when it is no longer required. Take the needle in and out of the fabric, making large stitches roughly the same length on both sides of the fabric. Use light-colored thread to avoid leaving marks.

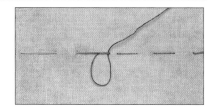

hemming stitches

A hem should be secured with neat, evenly spaced stitches that are almost invisible on the right side. Keep each stitch slightly loose. Pulling the thread too tight will disturb the surface of the fabric on the right side, making the hem more noticeable.

hemstitch

This stitch is used to secure a hem with a flat finished edge to flat fabric. Begin at a seam if possible, securing the thread on the edge of the hem.

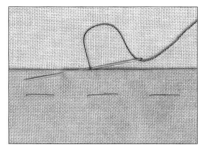

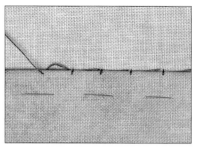

1. Using the tip of the needle, pick up one or two fabric threads on the garment and pull the thread through. Insert the needle through the hem edge, level with the emerging thread and ¼" from the first stitch.

2. Pull the thread through, leaving the stitch slightly loose. Continue stitching in the same manner until the hem is complete.

herringbone stitch

Most hemming stitches will break if the hem stretches out of shape. To minimize this, herringbone stitch can be used to secure hems or facings where some allowance for movement between the fabrics is necessary. This stitch gives with the fabric, which also makes it suitable for hems on knits. Work from left to right.

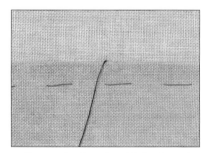

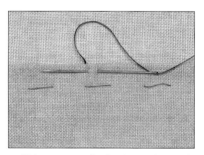

1. Secure the thread and bring it to the front on the edge of the hem.

2. Take a small horizontal stitch through the hem only, close to the edge of the hem.

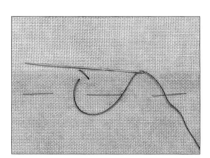

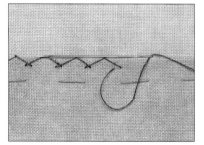

3. With the thread below the needle, take the same stitch ¼" to the right, picking up a few fabric threads on the garment level with the edge of the hem.

4. Repeat step 2, stitching ¼" to the right of the previous stitch. Continue in the same manner until the hem is complete.

slip stitch

This is the neatest method of securing a folded edge to flat fabric because the stitches are concealed in the fold on the wrong side and are almost invisible on the right side. Begin at a seam if possible.

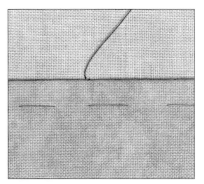

1. Secure the thread with backstitches in the fold of the hem.

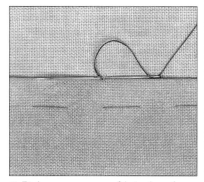

2. Pick up one or two fabric threads on the garment, level with the emerging thread on the hem.

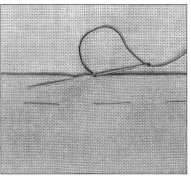

3. Pull the thread through. Slide the needle through the folded edge and emerge ¼" away.

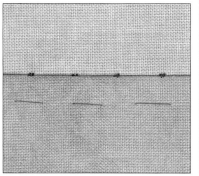

4. Pull the thread through, leaving the stitch slightly loose. Continue in the same manner until the hem is complete.

blind herringbone stitch

This stitch is worked between the two fabric layers and is invisible when the hem is pressed in position. It is worked similarly to the herringbone stitch, but the stitches are placed on the inside of the hem edge. The stitches must be positioned at the same level on the garment as they are on the hem to ensure the hem will remain at the measured depth.

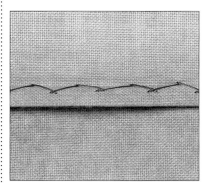

diagonal basting or tacking

When large areas need to be basted together quickly, work diagonal stitches in rows or as a filling. This technique is useful for holding pleats or nonfusible interfacing in place until they are permanently secured.

Bring the thread to the front on the lower left. Leaving a long diagonal stitch on the surface, take a large horizontal stitch through the fabric.

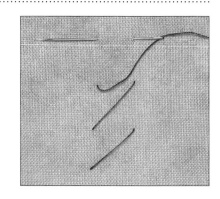

hems

A hem is a finished turned-under edge on the lower edge of any section of a garment. Choosing a hemming method will largely depend on the style of the garment and the fabric being used. For a professional result, a hem should always hang evenly and straight, without puckering around the stitching or the folded edge. Unless it is meant to be decorative, a hem should be inconspicuous. A simple turned-back, hand-stitched hem is the method most commonly used, but a hem can also be faced or bound.

Preparation

Accurate marking is the first step to achieve the best results. For straight skirts, dresses, tops, and pants, lay the garment on a flat surface and mark the hem allowance on the right side with pins. Fold under the hem along the pinned line and pin in place. Try the garment on and repin any adjustments. Lay the garment out flat again and trim off any excess fabric if necessary. Secure in place using one of the following methods.

finished flat edge

Finish the raw edge with a zigzag or overlock stitch. Secure the hem using your chosen method and press.

folded edge

Press under ¼" on the raw edge. Press the hem up and secure using your chosen method and press.

curved edge

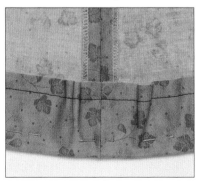

1. Work a row of machine easing (basting) ⅜" from the raw edge. Press under along the stitching line. Unfold.

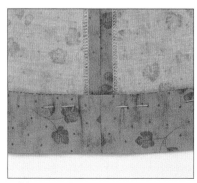

2. Trim ¼" from the fold line. Refold along the stitching line. Ease the folded hem to fit the flat fabric and pin in place. Hemstitch to secure. Press.

purchased bias binding

Bias binding is an effective hem finish for flared skirts because the bias adjusts to fit the curves without rippling. It's also a useful method for hemming thick fabrics. Use a narrow width of bias binding in a matching color.

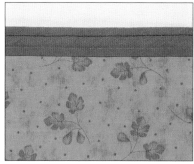

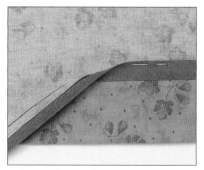

1. Unfold one edge of the binding. With right sides together, stitch the unfolded edge of the binding to the hem.

2. Press the binding away from the hem. Pin the hem in place and hemstitch or slip-stitch to secure. Press.

machine blind hem

Use the blind-hem presser foot and set the machine to a blind-hem stitch with the single zigzag stitches approximately ³⁄₈" apart. The width setting should be 2.5 or 3.

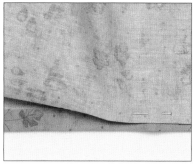

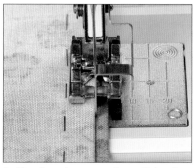

1. Finish or fold the raw edge. Place the garment with the right side facing up and fold back to reveal ³⁄₁₆" of hem edge. Pin and baste the layers together near the fold.

2. Keeping the center bar of the foot aligned with the fold, stitch the hem, catching a few threads of the garment with the zigzag stitches.

rolled hem

Rolled hems should be stitched starting at a raw edge at one side. Use the rolled-hem presser foot and set the machine to a medium-length straight stitch. A rolled hem is suitable for lightweight fabrics only and is the best option for sheer fabrics.

Trim away excess fabric from the hem allowances; only ¼"–³⁄₈" is needed for this type of hem.

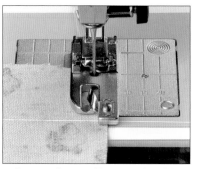

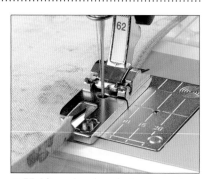

1. Lower the needle into the fabric edge. Work a few stitches, turning the flywheel by hand. Hold the threads at the back. Roll the fabric edge into the tunnel of the presser foot.

2. Holding the threads, begin sewing, guiding ¼"–³⁄₈" of the fabric folded in front of the foot. The depth of the fold will determine the finished width of the hem.

faced or false hem

A faced hem is not only useful to gain extra length in a garment, but it can also be invaluable to achieve a flat hem on a curved edge or to reduce bulk on a garment made from thick fabric.

Preparation

Stitch and finish all seams in the garment and facing.

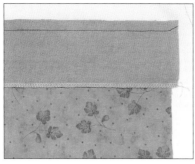

1. With right sides together and matching seams and centers, pin the facing to the garment edge. Stitch.

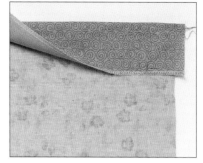

2. Trim the seam allowances and press to one side. Fold the facing to the inside, slightly rolling the seam to ensure the facing doesn't show on the right side of the garment. Secure the hem by hand or machine.

securing a faced corner

There are two ways to finish a hem where it meets a faced opening. The first will allow the hem to be adjusted if required, but is a bit bulkier. The second is permanently fixed; you can't let down the hem because part of it will be trimmed away to reduce bulk. The instructions show an attached facing, but the method is the same if using an integrated facing.

method 1

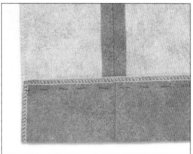

1. Press any seam allowances open. Pin the hem in position and baste in place. Secure the hem by hand or machine.

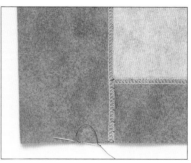

2. Fold the facing to the wrong side. Aligning the lower edges, stitch the edge closed and the facing to the hem.

method 2

1. Mark the hem fold line. Fold facing right sides together with garment, stitch across the lower edge just below the line. Trim the lower edge and clip the corner.

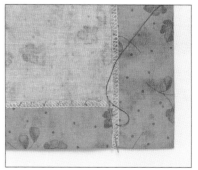

2. Turn the facing right side out. Hand stitch the hem and the facing edge to the hem.

hems

interfacing

Interfacing is a thin layer of fabric attached to the wrong side of the main garment fabric to give body to an area of the garment that needs to retain a crisp shape, such as a collar or cuffs, or to add stability to an area that may take much stress, such as a button band or front facing. Interfacing comes in a variety of weights, and some are fusible while others are not. The type of interfacing you choose depends on the garment fabric you're using and the purpose the interfacing is serving.

non-fusible interfacing

Non-fusible interfacing is held in place on the wrong side of the garment fabric with basting, which remains in place until after the garment pieces are joined and pressed. Ensure that the basting is clearly visible from the right side because you will not be able to access it from the inside.

heavyweight non-fusible interfacing

Heavyweight interfacings add bulk, so cut away the seam allowances and the hems on all edges of the interfacing pieces before attaching them.

1. Aligning the edges with seam lines, baste the interfacing to the wrong side of the fabric just inside the edge. Work diagonal tacking in the center, to keep interfacing flat.

2. Work herringbone stitch around the edge of the interfacing, stitching through the seam allowance and catching the interfacing only.

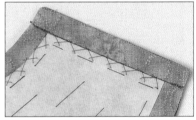

3. Pin the garment pieces right sides together. Stitch along the edge of the interfacing, catching the herringbone stitches in the seam.

lightweight non-fusible interfacing

Since lightweight interfacings do not add a great amount of bulk to a seam, the interfacing is cut the same size as the garment piece.

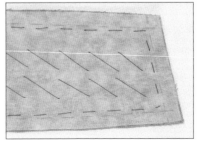

1. Aligning edges, baste the interfacing to the wrong side of the garment piece as described above.

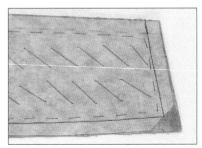

2. With right sides together, pin the garment pieces together. Stitch along seam line. Trim interfacing at the corners.

fusible interfacing

Fusible interfacing comes in many weights. It has a heat-activated adhesive coating on one surface, which bonds to the fabric. The adhesive side is the wrong side. Always test the interfacing on a scrap of the garment fabric first. Unsuitable fabrics for use with fusible interfacing include velvet and some textured fabrics like seersucker. Cut out the garment and corresponding interfacing pieces according to the pattern, ensuring the adhesive side of each interfacing piece will face the wrong side of the fabric. Transfer any pattern markings to the right side of the interfacing.

heavyweight fusible interfacing

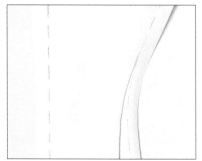

1. To prevent bulk in the seams, trim the seam allowances just outside the stitching line.

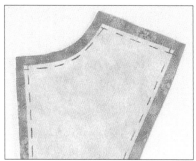

2. Aligning seam lines, fuse the interfacing to the wrong side of the garment piece.

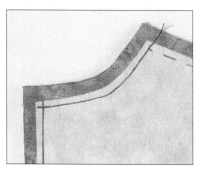

3. With right sides together, pin the garment pieces together. Stitch along the seam lines.

lightweight fusible interfacing

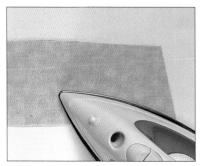

1. Because lightweight interfacing adds little bulk, you don't need to trim the seam allowances. Align the edges and fuse the interfacing to the wrong side of the garment piece.

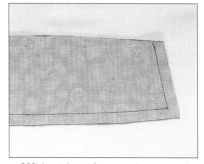

2. With right sides together, pin the garment pieces together. Stitch along the seam line.

linings

A lining is applied to the inside of a garment to add to its structure and conceal the seams and interfacing. It is most often made from a slippery fabric to allow the garment to slide easily over other clothing.

A lining can either be secured on all edges within the garment or it can be free-hanging, floating inside the garment, suspended from the shoulders or a waistband.

Half linings can also be applied to the upper half of a skirt or trousers to provide support at the front or to stop the main fabric from "bagging" at the back when seated.

If a garment is finished with a secured lining, the seams don't need to be finished because they won't be subjected to abrasion when concealed by the lining.

Darts and seams should always be situated in the same place on the lining as they are on the outer layer. Some exceptions are small pleats and easing that are often part of the lining to allow for movement when the garment is worn. Construction details such as darts should always be pressed in the same direction on the lining as they are on the outer layer.

An interlining is a separate layer of fabric or interfacing, which is applied to the wrong side of the main fabric. Both layers are basted together around the outer edge and treated as one layer during construction.

edge-to-edge lining

This type of lining is a mirror image of the outer layer and is attached along the outer edges. Methods for attaching this style of lining will vary depending on the style of garment. Refer to your pattern instructions.

Preparation

Cut out all garment pieces, and then cut a copy of each main piece from lining fabric. You don't need to cut lining pieces for waistbands or facings.

1. Layer each garment and lining piece to ensure they match. Trim any edges if necessary.

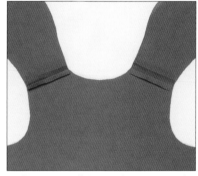

2. Construct all internal seams on the garment, leaving an opening at each side seam. Repeat for the lining pieces.

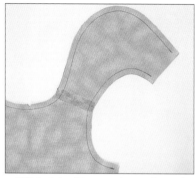

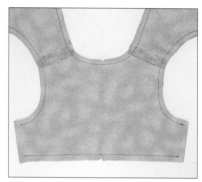

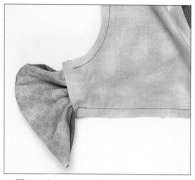

3. With right sides together and matching raw edges, seams, and markings, pin and stitch the lining to the garment around the outer edges. Begin and end at the marked points.

4. Repeat on the lower edge of the back.

5. Trim the seam allowances and clip or notch the curves. Turn the garment to the right side through a side-seam opening.

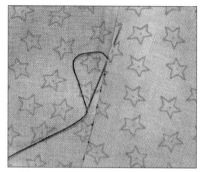

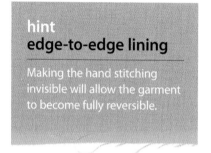

hint
edge-to-edge lining

Making the hand stitching invisible will allow the garment to become fully reversible.

6. With right sides together, stitch and finish the garment and lining side seams in the same manner as the facing shoulder seams, steps 5–8 on page 81.

7. Roll the seams to the outer edge and press.

free-hanging lining

A free-hanging lining is a duplicate layer of the outer fabric section that "floats" inside a garment. It's secured on the inside of the upper edge. The lower edges are hemmed separately, allowing the lining to move independently. This type of lining is commonly used on skirts, dresses, and coats.

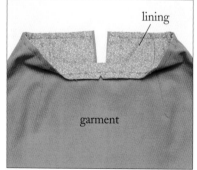

lining

garment

1. Construct the outer and lining layers of the garment separately. If necessary, insert a zipper into the outer garment layer.

2. Turn the outer garment layer right side out. With wrong sides together, slide the lining into the outer layer. Matching centers, seams, and markings, baste the layers together on upper edge.

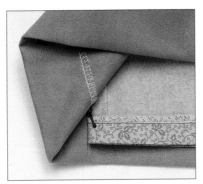

3. Fold under the opening on the lining to align with the stitching. Pin and hand stitch in place. Attach the waistband.

4. Hem the garment. Press. Repeat for the lining, making it 1¼" shorter than the garment. At each side seam, attach the lining to the garment with a ¾" thread loop.

faced lining

A lining is often formed with a facing at the leading edge to ensure it remains hidden. The facing is made from the same fabric as the outer garment.

Preparation

On the pattern piece for the outer layer, mark a line a short distance away from the opening edge. Cut through the line and make new pattern pieces, adding at least ⅜" on each side of the cut edge for the seam allowance.

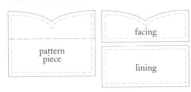

Cut the pieces for the outer layer using the original pattern piece. Cut the facings and the lining using the new pattern pieces.

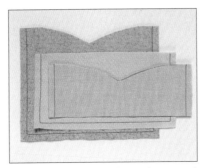

1. Construct the outer layer, facing, and lining separately.

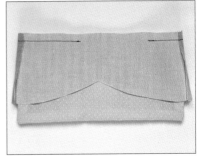

2. Trim the seam allowances and press open. With right sides together and leaving an opening, pin and stitch the lower edge of the facing to the upper edge of the lining.

3. Trim the seam allowances and press the facing away from the lining. With right sides together and matching seams, pin and stitch the lining to the garment.

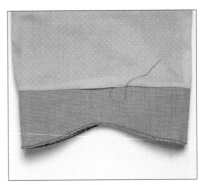

4. Turn right side out through the opening. Roll the seam to the edge. Topstitch or edgestitch to secure the facing. Hand stitch the opening closed.

necklines

Necklines can be finished with binding, a facing, or a collar.

See also "Attaching Collars" on pages 66–70 and "Combination Facing" on page 80.

bound neckline

When using a pattern where the neckline is not specifically designed for a bound edge, it's necessary to trim away the seam allowance before attaching the binding. See "Armholes" on page 32 for more information on bound edges. The following instructions are for attaching a single binding, but double binding would work just as well.

Preparation

Prepare the neckline by stitching and pressing the shoulder seams. Attach or construct any facings or linings along the opening edge. Attach any decorative elements such as piping, lace, keyholes, or front button tabs. Mark the center front and back on the neckline.

overlapping

With this technique, the binding overlaps at the back button band, creating bulk at that point. This method is suitable for light- to mediumweight fabrics only. Prepare the garment as described above and baste the facing or lining in place at the neckline.

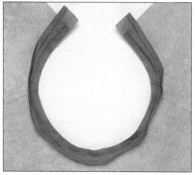

1. With right sides together and matching raw edges along the neckline, pin the binding in place, allowing a seam allowance to extend at both ends. Stitch.

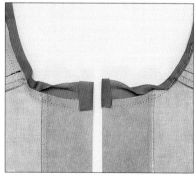

2. Fold under the seam allowance at the ends of the binding. Fold the binding to the wrong side, enclosing the seam allowance. Pin and baste the fold so that it just covers the previous stitching line.

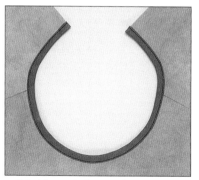

3. Machine stitch on the right side along the edge of the binding. Press.

butted binding

With this technique the ends of the binding butt together at the center back, allowing just the extensions on the button closure to overlap. It is suitable for heavier-weight fabrics and for necklines finished with lace or fabric ruffles.

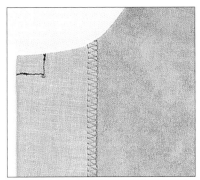

1. Fold the back bodice and facing right sides together at the upper edge. Stitch along the center back neckline for the width of the binding. Pivot and stitch to the folded edge.

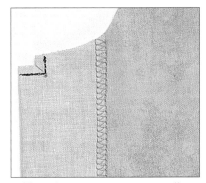

2. Trim, leaving a narrow seam allowance. Clip the inner corner.

hint
ready-made binding

Using ready-made binding, unfold one edge and use this edge to attach the binding, following the fold line as a guide for the stitching

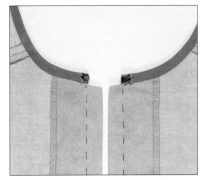

3. Turn the facing right side out. Pushing out the corner, baste the facing in place. Attach the binding following steps 1–3 on page 99. Stitch a hook and loop at the ends of the binding.

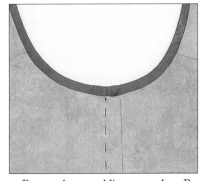

4. Press the neckline gently. By eliminating the overlapped binding, the bulk at the back neckline is reduced and a flatter finish is achieved.

necklines

faced necklines

Almost any shape, from a simple round neck to more complicated scallops and keyholes, can be built into the neckline using a facing. Neckline facings are usually separate pieces of the garment fabric, but may be cut from lighter-weight fabric to reduce bulk. They are cut on the same grain and mirror the shape at the neckline and openings of the garment pieces. Although the pattern you have chosen may have a different neckline shape than the one shown, all facings are constructed in a similar manner. See page 80 for a combined neck and armhole facing. See page 68 for using a facing to attach a collar.

Preparation

Apply interfacing to the wrong side of the facing pieces. Stay stitch just inside the neckline seam allowance of the garment pieces.

simple faced neckline

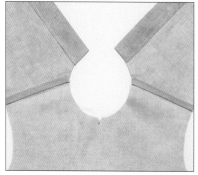

1. With right sides together, pin, stitch, and finish the bodice seams. Construct any separate facings, such as along the front openings here.

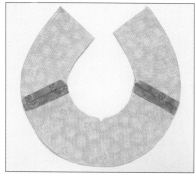

2. With right sides together, join the facing pieces at the shoulders. Trim the seam allowances and press open. Finish the outer raw edge.

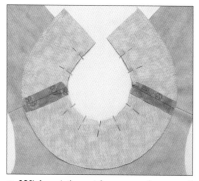

3. With right sides together and matching seams, centers, and raw edges along the neckline, pin the facing in place.

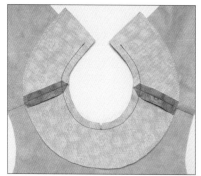

4. With the facing on top, begin at the center and stitch around one half of the neckline at a time.

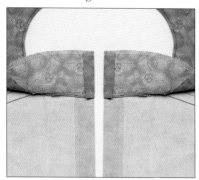

5. Trim and grade the seam allowances. Clip the curves. Press the facing and seam allowances away from the garment. Understitch the seam on the facing. Press under the seam allowances on both sides of the opening.

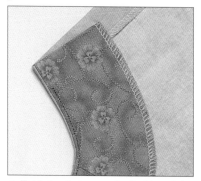

6. Fold the facing to the inside of the garment and press. Hand stitch the edge of the facing to the opening edge and shoulder seams.

combined neck and front opening

For this type of facing, the back neck and front opening facings are sewn together to form a continuous piece. The following instructions show a front opening, but the opening could alternatively be at the back.

Preparation

Apply interfacing to the wrong side of the facing pieces. Stay stitch just inside the neckline seam allowance of the garment pieces.

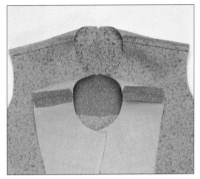

1. Prepare the garment and facing following steps 1 and 2 on page 101.

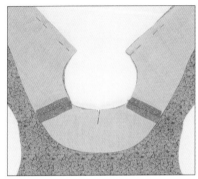

2. With right sides together and matching raw edges, seams, and centers, pin and baste the facing to the neckline and opening.

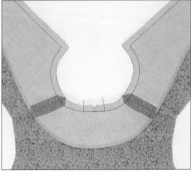

3. Beginning at the center, stitch around the neckline and down one side of the opening. Then, with the garment on top, return to the center and complete the seam.

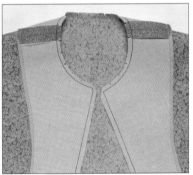

4. Trim and grade the seam allowances if necessary. Clip the curves and corners.

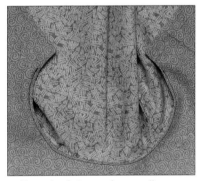

5. Press the facing and seam allowances away from the garment. Understitch the seam on the facing, beginning and ending close to the corner point. Do this along the neckline as well as on each front opening edge.

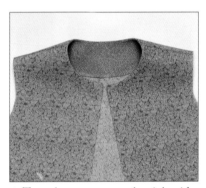

6. Turn the garment to the right side. Press. Hand stitch the edge of the facing to the garment shoulder seams.

placket opening

A simple placket is a neat way to create a partial neckline opening. The following instructions allow for a 1"-wide placket, suitable for adult garments. Ensure the opening is deep enough to allow the garment to slip over the head.

Preparation

Fold the front bodice in half and finger-press the center front. Measure and mark a line from the neckline along the fold, ⅜" shorter than the opening.

Cut a ¼"-wide slit on the marked line. Stitch and finish the shoulder seams. Prepare the garment and neckline following step 1 on page 101. Cut two placket pieces, each 2¾" wide and ¾" longer than the finished opening. Apply interfacing to half the width of each piece, ensuring you have a left and a right piece.

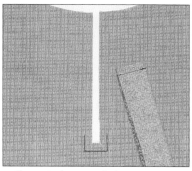

1. Stay stitch around the opening on the front and clip diagonally into the corners. Fold the placket pieces in half, right sides together. Stitch across the upper ends.

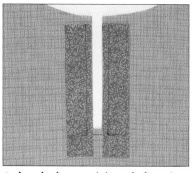

3. Attach the remaining placket piece in the same manner to the opposite side of the opening. Mark the stitching line across the lower edge.

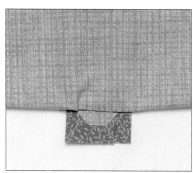

5. Repeat for the other placket piece. Fold the garment to expose the ends of the placket. Stitch through all layers, taking care not to catch the garment body in the seam.

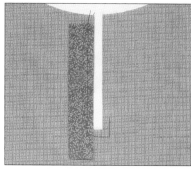

2. Trim the placket seam allowances and clip the corner. Turn right side out. With right sides together, align the finished placket end with the neckline seam line. Matching raw edges at the opening, pin and stitch along the length of the placket, finishing at the base of the opening.

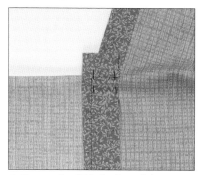

4. Rotate the folded edge of the upper placket counterclockwise to match the opposite seam line.

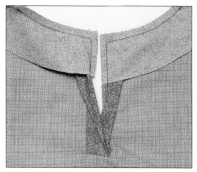

6. Finish the placket seams. Attach the neck facing, keeping the upper edges of the placket out of the way, stitching along the previous opening seam lines.

7. Trim and clip the seam allowances and corners. Press the seam allowances toward the facing and understitch. Press and hand stitch the facing to the garment shoulder seams.

necklines

103

piping

Piping is a narrow fabric trim inserted into a seam to strengthen and define an edge. It can be either flat or corded, with the fabric cut on the straight grain or on the bias. See pages 39–41 for cutting and joining lengths of bias fabric.

The width or thickness of the piping should always be in keeping with the scale of the project—extra fine for babies' and children's wear up to the heavy corded piping used in upholstery and soft furnishing items.

Flat piping consists of a fabric strip folded in half wrong sides together along the length and pressed flat. The width of the strip is calculated as twice the width of the finished piping plus twice the required seam allowance. It's inserted into a seam in the same manner as corded piping.

Corded piping is constructed by sewing a length of twisted cotton cord inside the tunnel of a strip of fabric cut on the bias. To determine the width of the fabric strip, sandwich a piece of piping in the looped end of a tape measure. Wrap the tape measure around the cord until it extends by the seam allowance you will be using. The amount of piping needed will equal the measurement along the edge to be piped, adding extra to go around corners and to join the piping into a continuous length if necessary.

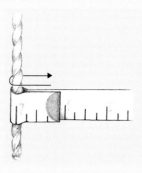

making corded piping

1. Cut and construct a continuous length of bias strip following the steps on page 39. Lay the cord along the center of the strip on the wrong side.

2. With wrong sides together and matching raw edges, fold the fabric over the cord. Stitch as close to the cord as possible using a zipper foot.

hint **piping**

If the depth of the piping seam allowance is different than the seam allowance you are using, match the stitching line on the piping to the stitching line on the garment piece.

attaching piping to a straight edge

1. Matching stitching lines, pin the piping to the right side of the garment piece. Stitch along the piping stitching line.

2. Matching raw edges, pin the remaining fabric piece over the piping. Baste the layers together within the seam allowance. Stitch between the previous stitching line and the corded edge of the piping.

3. Trim the seam allowances. Turn to the right side. To place the piping on the edge, understitch the seam on the back. Press carefully, taking care not to crush the piping.

attaching piping to a curved edge

Preparation

Clip the piping seam allowance at even intervals—the tighter the curve, the closer the clips.

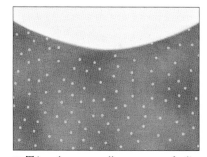

1. Concave curve. Matching stitching lines, pin and baste the piping to the right side of the garment, shaping it to fit the curve. Stitch along the piping stitching line.

2. Matching raw edges, pin remaining fabric piece over piping. Tack the layers together within the seam allowance. Stitch between the previous stitching line and the corded edge of the piping.

3. Trim the seam allowances and clip the curve. Understitch the seam if needed. Fold with the piping on the outer edge and press carefully, taking care not to crush the piping.

4. Convex curve. The instructions are the same as for concave curves except that the curve is notched rather than clipped.

hint piping

To eliminate excess bulk in seams that cross the ends of a piping strip, remove the cord from the end of the piping to the seam line. Pinch the end of the cord between your fingers and carefully ease the fabric back until the desired length of cord is exposed. Trim off the cord and ease the fabric back into position. Without being secured at the ends, the cord will float within the tube.

piping

piping a sharp corner

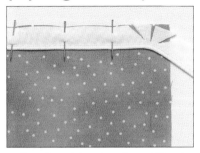

1. Pin the piping in place. Clip the piping seam allowance to the stitching at the corner point. Clip diagonally on either side of the corner.

2. Turn the piping around the corner, allowing the clipped seam allowance to open. Stitch along the piping stitching line.

attaching continuous piping

When piping is required around a complete shape such as a cushion or sleeve band, join the piping at the point where the ends meet, either in an inconspicuous spot or aligned with a seam.

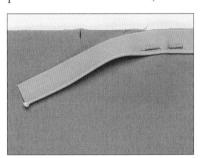

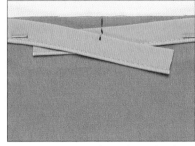

1. Method one. Mark a point for the join on the edge of the fabric. Begin pinning the piping to the fabric, allowing 1¼" to extend past the mark.

2. Pin piping around the shape, finishing with the end extending past the starting point. Mark the edge of both piping ends even with the mark on the fabric.

3. Unpick the piping stitching for 3" at the ends. Measure and cut off excess cord at the marked point allowing ³⁄₈" (or more) to overlap. Bind and secure.

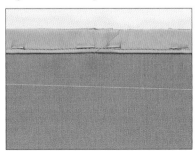

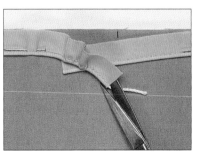

4. Trim excess piping fabric and stitch the join, following the instructions on page 41. Reposition the cord and replace the stitching. Re-pin the piping to the fabric edge.

1. Method two. Mark the join on the fabric seam allowance. Pin the piping to the fabric, allowing 1¼" to extend past the mark. Carefully pull the cord out and trim even with the mark.

2. Overlap the piping seam allowances at the mark, curving the ends into the seam and pin. Stitch the piping to the fabric. Trim the ends.

plackets

A placket is a functional detail that finishes a partial opening in a garment, such as a sleeve opening above a cuff.

hemmed placket

Preparation

At the required position, mark a line ⅜" longer than the finished length of the opening, at a right angle to the raw edge. Cut along the line.

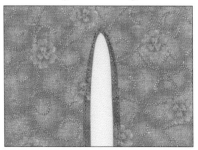

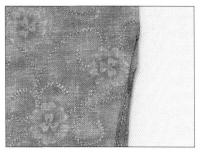

1. Fold and stitch narrow double-folded hems on both sides of the opening, tapering at the point of the opening.

2. With right sides together, align the hemmed edges. Stitch a tiny dart.

3. Press the dart to one side at the end of the placket.

faced placket

Preparation

At the required position, mark a cutting line slightly shorter than the desired finished length of the opening, at a right angle to the raw edge of the fabric. Cut a rectangle for the facing in proportion to the size of the opening. Mark the same line, centered on the lower edge of the facing. Finish the outer edge of the facing. Cut along the line on the garment and the facing.

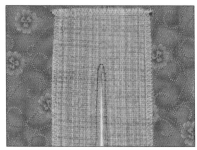

1. With right sides together and matching lines, pin the facing in place. Stitch along both sides of the opening, beginning and ending ³⁄₁₆" from the edge and tapering to a point above the cut.

2. Clip the seam allowances at the cut end. Press the seam allowances and facing away from the opening. Fold the facing to the inside. Edgestitch around the opening. Hand stitch the outer edges of the facing to secure. Press.

2a. Alternatively, tack the facing in position and topstitch from the right side, placing the stitching an even distance from the opening.

107

lapped placket

This type of placket uses a narrow fabric binding for the raw edge of the opening. The number of fabric layers makes it unsuitable for thick fabrics.

Preparation

Cut a strip for the placket that is twice the finished width plus two seam allowances and double the length of the opening.

seamed opening

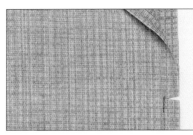

1. Stitch the seam, leaving an opening for the desired length of the placket. Clip the seam allowances, angling the cut to the end of the stitching.

2. Finish the seam to the clipped point and press to one side. Spread the opening. With right sides together, pin the placket strip along the opening. Stitch, just catching the finished end of the seam. Finish the placket following steps 3–5 below.

unseamed opening

For an unseamed opening, crease a fold at a right angle to the raw edge at the position for the opening on the garment. Mark a line on the fold for the required depth of the placket.

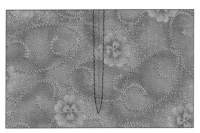

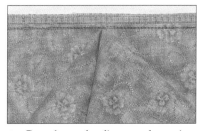

1. Stay stitch along both sides of the line beginning and ending $1/8$" from the raw edge and tapering to a point above the line.

2. Cut along the line to the point. Spread the cut edges. With right sides together, position the stay stitching just above the stitching line on the placket. Pin and stitch.

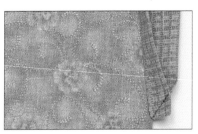

3. Press seam toward the placket and press under the remaining seam allowances on the placket. Fold the placket to the wrong side and hand stitch.

4. Press. On the wrong side, fold the placket in half, matching folded edges. Stitch diagonally across the end.

5. Depending on the overlap, left over right or vice versa, press one placket under to wrong side of garment and leave the other extending.

pleats

Pleats are measured folds created in the edge of the fabric. Unlike gathering, pleats are a structured, flat method of controlling fullness. They can be pressed into crisp creases or hang as soft folds. The folds in a pleat can be edgestitched to make them permanent or just one section topstitched to hold the pleat in position.

For soft unpressed pleats, almost any fabric can be used successfully, but some fabrics hold crisp pleats better than others. Pleats hang more effectively and hold their shape longer if they are folded on the straight grain. Cut the fabric strictly on the grain for multiple pleats, or try to fold an isolated pleat as close to the grain as possible.

The three main types of pleats are knife-edged, box, and inverted. Inverted and box pleats are the reverse side of the same fold formation.

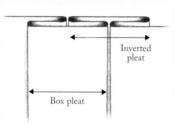

Inverted pleat

Box pleat

Pleats are formed by taking a fold line to meet a placement line. It is often better to use a pattern just to mark the positions of the lines on the top edge of the fabric. With the pattern removed, mark the lines with basting following the threads in the fabric. Choose different-colored threads for the fold lines and placement lines to make them more distinct. Work on the right side to make it easier to match fabric patterns such as plaids.

folded pleats
knife-edged pleats

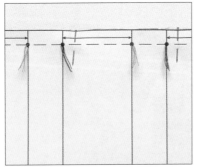

1. With the pattern piece still in place, use tailor's tacks to mark the fold and placement positions on the upper edge.

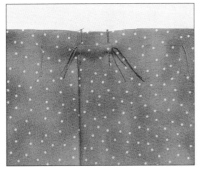

2. Take the fold mark to meet the placement mark for the first pleat and pin both sides of the pleat.

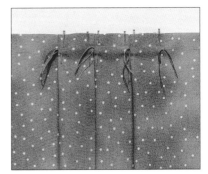

3. Repeat for any remaining pleats.

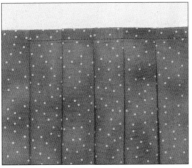

4. Baste the folds in place just inside the stitching line. Press lightly from the wrong side along the upper edge.

4a. Mark, fold, and pin the pleats along the length following the grain. Tack in place. Press when the garment is complete.

hint pleating

If you have a number of pleats to form, make a cardboard or plastic pleating gauge to make consistent measuring easier.

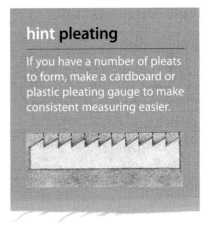

inverted pleat

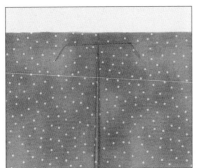

1. A pair of knife-edged pleats folded toward each other creates an inverted pleat.

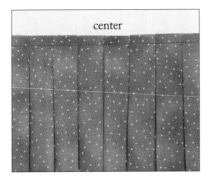

center

2. Knife-edged pleats folded in opposite directions form an inverted pleat at the center.

box pleat

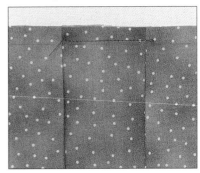

A box pleat is formed when two knife-edged pleats are folded away from each other.

stitched pleats
knife-edged pleats

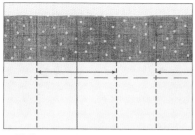 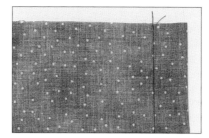 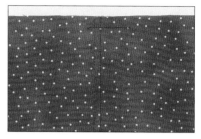

1. Following the grain of the fabric, mark the center fold line and the left stitching line of each pleat on the wrong side of the fabric. Mark the end points.

2. Fold the pleat with right sides together along the fold line. Stitch to the lower end point of the pleat.

3. On the right side, position the pleat and press. Baste the top edge. Topstitch the pleat ¼" from the seamed edge. At the lower end, stitch diagonally to the end of the pleat.

inverted pleats

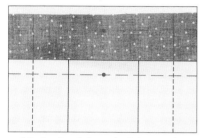 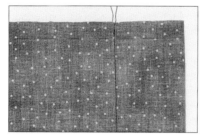 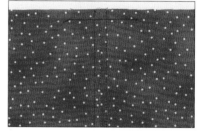

1. Mark the left and right stitching lines and the center on the wrong side of the fabric. Mark the end points.

2. Matching stitching lines, fold the pleat right sides together on the center mark. Stitch to the lower end point of the pleat.

3. Pin the pleat, matching the center mark to the stitching line. Press. Topstitch along both sides, close to the fold and forming a point at the lower end.

box pleats

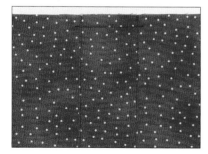

Form the pleat on the right side of the fabric in a similar manner to an inverted pleat. Topstitch along each side close to the fold.

hints pleating

Check the fit before topstitching any pleats.

The end of a stitched pleat is an area of great strain when the garment is worn. Stitch as securely as possible at this point.

To set the pleats, keep the basting in place until after the garment is finished. Fold and secure the hem before pressing pleats into their final position at the lower edge of a skirt.

To prevent ridges on the right side, lay strips of thin cardboard under the pleats when pressing after the garment is complete.

pockets

Pockets first appeared as small concealed pouches to carry a handkerchief or a few coins. Over time, pockets have evolved into a myriad of forms that are not only functional, but become part of the styling of a garment. Pockets can have a tailored or casual appearance, depending on their construction.

unlined patch pockets

A patch pocket is attached to the outside of the garment with machine stitching. Patch pockets can be lined or unlined, plain or decorated, in basic or novelty shapes.

Preparation

Check the position of the pocket to ensure it's at a comfortable height. Adjust if necessary. Mark the pocket position using tailor's tacks, basting, or a fabric marker appropriate for the fabric. Apply interfacing where required to add strength and stability.

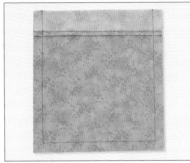

1. Square corners. Turn under a narrow hem, stitch, and press. Then refold the hem toward the right side of the fabric. Stitch the around the sides and bottom of the pocket just a hair inside the seam line. Trim the seam and clip the corners along the hemmed edges.

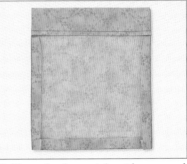

2. Turn the hem right side out and re-press the hem; also press under the seam allowances on the sides and bottom using the stitching as a guide.

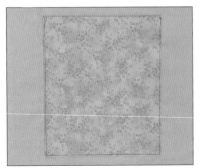

3. Baste the pocket in place on the garment. Beginning and ending with a triangle of stitching, at the top corners, edgestitch in place, leaving the top edge open.

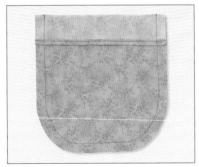

1. Rounded corners. Fold and stitch the upper hem as for square-cornered pockets, stitching around the sides and bottom of the pocket.

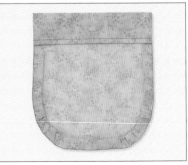

2. Using a straight pin, gently pull on the stitching to roll the curved corners to the wrong side. The stitching should be just inside the fold. Press under the seam allowances and then stitch in place as for square-cornered pockets.

patch pockets with flaps

A flap usually has the same styling as the pocket it is paired with. The following instructions show a flap with a rounded lower edge to match the pocket on the sample. Although other flaps may have a different shape, the method of attaching them is the same. Flaps may also be attached without a pocket, as a design feature. They can also conceal the bound opening of an internal slashed pocket.

Preparation

Form and attach the pocket following the instructions, opposite. Mark a line ⅜" above the pocket.

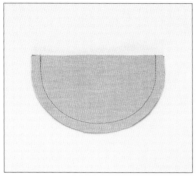

1. Apply interfacing to one flap piece. With right sides together and matching raw edges, pin the flap pieces together. Stitch around the sides and lower edge.

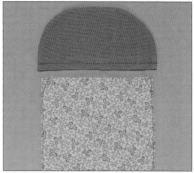

2. Trim and grade the seam allowances and clip the curves. Turn right side out and press. With the flap facing away from the pocket, pin and stitch in place, aligning the stitching line on the flap with the marked line.

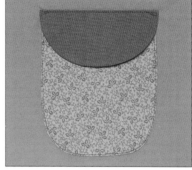

3. Trim the seam allowances and clip the corners. Fold the flap down to cover the pocket. Stitch across the top of the flap, matching the stitching on the pocket.

hints patch pockets

To reinforce the stress points on the garment, fuse a piece of interfacing onto the garment fabric behind the upper corners of the pocket before stitching the pocket in position.

Triangular corner reinforcement

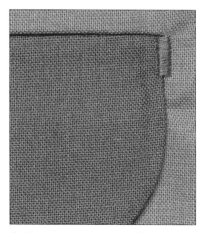

Satin stitch corner reinforcement

hip pocket

Front hip pockets are inserted into a seam at the sides and attached under a waistband along the upper edge. The upper edge of the pocket and the amount of fabric showing behind the opening can be designed in many ways, but this style of pocket still consists of two main pieces, the pocket front and the pocket back.

1. Apply a strip of interfacing to the wrong side of the pocket front along the pocket opening edge.

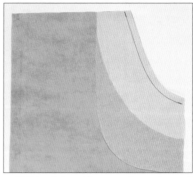

2. With right sides together, pin and stitch the pocket front to the garment piece along the edge.

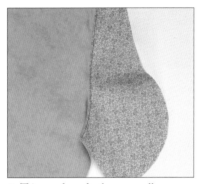

3. Trim and grade the seam allowances and clip the curve. Press the seam allowances toward the pocket front and understitch close to the seam.

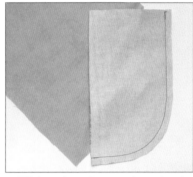

4. With right sides together, pin the pocket back to the outer edge of the pocket front. Stitch.

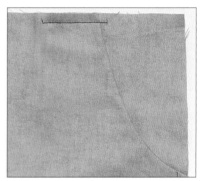

5. Trim and finish the seam. Matching raw edges and marks, place all layers together at the top edge and baste in place.

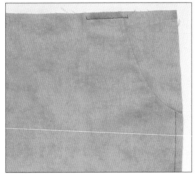

6. Repeat at the side. The front of the garment is now ready to have the back attached at the sides.

hints pockets

The pocket opening must be big enough for the hand to comfortably enter without placing too much strain on the attachment points.

If you have changed the position of a pocket, be sure to transfer alterations to all pattern pieces involved.

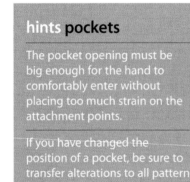

in-seam pockets

In-seam pockets can be constructed in different ways. In a separate in-seam pocket, additional pocket pieces are attached to the side seam of the garment. The pockets can be cut from lighter-weight fabric to reduce bulk inside the garment. In that case, cut a small facing of the garment fabric and attach it to the pocket opening to ensure the different fabric won't show, if the pocket gapes open.

An integrated in-seam pocket is cut as part of the main garment piece, so the seam is continuous along the side of the garment and around the pocket.

separate in-seam pocket

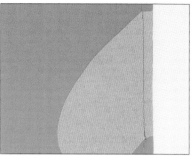

1. With right sides together and matching markings, pin a pocket piece to a garment piece. Stitch. Repeat for the remaining pocket and garment piece.

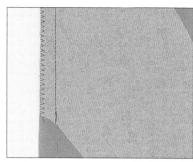

2. Finish the seam allowances for the depth of the pocket.

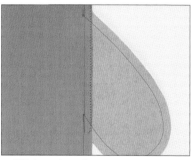

3. With right sides together, matching raw edges and markings, pin and stitch the garment and pocket pieces together, excluding the pocket opening.

4. Trim and finish the seam allowances. Press the pocket toward the front of the garment. Reinforce the upper and lower ends of the opening, if desired.

integrated in-seam pocket

Preparation

Stitch staytape along the front opening edge of the pocket extension, just inside the seam line.

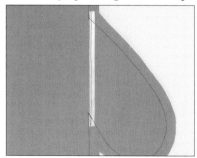

1. With right sides together and matching raw edges, pin the two garment pieces together. Stitch the side and pocket seams continuously.

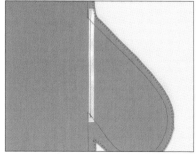

2. Reinforce the stitching at top and bottom points of the pocket. Trim the pocket seams and then finish the edges of the garment and pocket seams.

3. Press the pocket toward the front of the garment. Reinforce the upper and lower ends of the opening if desired.

slash pockets

Another form of pocket is constructed with a pocket bag on the inside of the garment that is accessed through a slash made in the garment. The cuts can be horizontal or slanted depending on the desired styling. The cut edges are finished with flaps or welts which are the only parts of the pockets visible on the outside of the garment.

pocket opening

Preparation

As with bound buttonholes, attention to detail in the marking and construction of these pockets is important to achieve a professional look. Mark the cutting line for the pocket on the right side of the fabric.

Welt pockets

Besom pockets

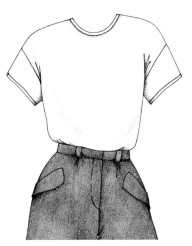

Slash pockets with flaps

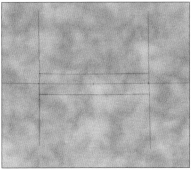

1. Mark lines at each end of the cutting line at right angles to the center line. Extend all lines 1½" past the cutting line. Mark another line $5/16$" above and below the center line.

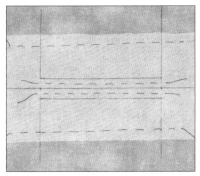

2. Repeat the markings on a piece of lightweight non-fusible interfacing and place it behind the opening. Pin and baste around the outer edge and close to the center line on both sides.

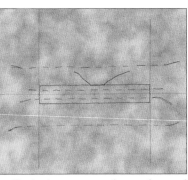

3. Beginning on one long edge and pivoting at the corners, stay stitch around the opening.

hints slashed pockets

Use a short stitch length.

Press carefully after each step. Leaving pressing to the final step will not set sharp edges.

Take the same number of stitches across both pocket ends to ensure the distances are even.

besom pocket

A besom (or double-welt) pocket adds a neat tailored finish to a pocket opening.

Preparation

Prepare the pocket opening on the garment piece. Cut two pocket pieces with rounded lower edges, each 1" wider than the finished pocket opening. Cut one piece the desired depth plus 2¾". Cut the second the desired depth plus 1¼".

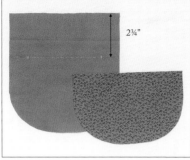

1. Mark a cutting line across the wrong side of the larger pocket piece at the desired depth. Rotate the pocket pieces before attaching them to the garment.

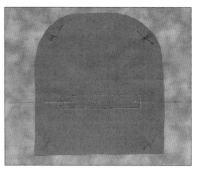

2. Matching the pocket line with the center line, pin the large pocket to the garment, right sides together. Then, with the garment on top, stitch just outside the stay stitching. Cut the center line and clip diagonally into the corners.

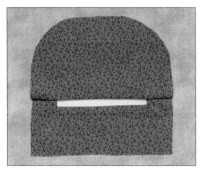

3. Push the pocket through to the wrong side of the garment. Roll the seam to the edge of the rectanglar opening. Press. Fold the upper section down to form a pleat with the fold in the center of the opening. Press.

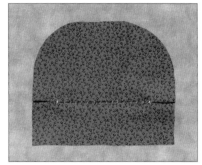

4. Fold the lower pocket section up to form another pleat in the same manner as before. Press. From the right side, secure the edges with basting. Baste through the pleats near the stitching.

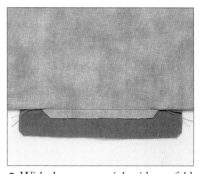

5. With the garment right side up, fold the garment piece back to expose one edge of the pocket. Stitch across the opening's seam allowance. Repeat on the remaining three edges of the opening. Press.

6. Stitch the remaining smaller pocket piece to the straight edge of the large pocket. Trim and finish the seam.

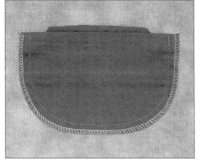

7. Fold the large pocket piece down. Trim the lower edges even with the smaller piece, if necessary. Pin the two layers together, stitch around the raw edges, and finish edges.

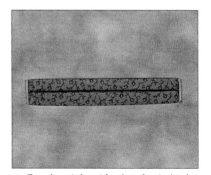

8. On the right side, hand stitch the ends to secure or stitch a bartack through all layers.

simple welt pockets

A welt is a band of fabric attached to the lower edge of the pocket opening.

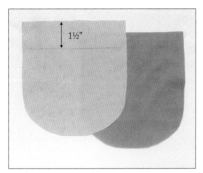

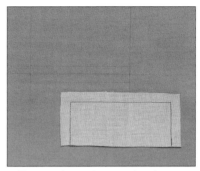

1. Cut two pocket pieces, each 1" wider than the finished pocket width and 1½" wider than the desired depth. Mark a line across the wrong side of one pocket piece at the desired depth.

2. Prepare the pocket opening (see page 116). Interface one welt piece. Pin the two welt pieces right sides together. Stitch each end and one long edge, pivoting at the corners.

3. Trim the seam allowances and clip the corners. Turn to the right side. Trim the seam allowances on the raw edges to $5/16$" and clip the corners. Baste the raw edges together.

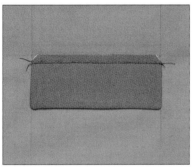

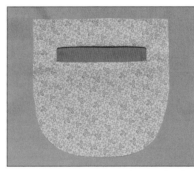

4. With the interfaced side of the welt facing the right side of the garment, pin and baste the welt to the lower edge of the marked opening.

5. Sandwiching the welt, stitch the marked pocket piece to the garment, following steps 2 and 3 on page 117, omitting the pleat.

6. Attach the second pocket piece and finish the pocket following steps 6 and 7 on page 117. Press.

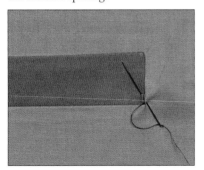

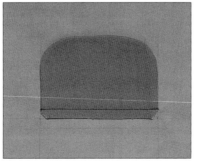

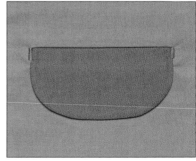

7. On the right side, fold the welt up to cover the opening. Hand stitch the sides to the garment or edgestitch through all layers. Press.

8. Optional pocket flap. Construct a flap and prepare a pocket opening as for the welt pocket. With the flap facing upward, baste along the upper pocket stitching line.

9. Finish the pocket following steps 6 and 7 on page 117. On the right side, hand stitch or edgestitch the sides through all layers.

ruffles

Ruffles are decorative strips of fabric, gathered or eased into a seam or along a hem to produce fullness at the outer edge. Ruffles can be cut from a straight length of fabric and gathered, or cut from a donut shape with a much larger outer curve than the inner curve. The gathered ruffle can have one or both edges finished with a plain narrow hem, or with a variety of decorative trims such as lace, braid, or ribbon. To determine the length of fabric needed for a gathered ruffle, allow three times the finished length for full ruffles and twice the length for a softly gathered ruffle. It may be necessary to cut several strips of fabric and sew them together to achieve the right length.

plain ruffle

Preparation

Cut a strip of fabric the desired finished depth of the ruffle, plus seam and hem allowances. Finish the hem.

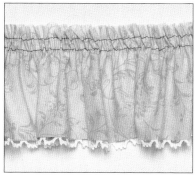

1. Stitch two rows of machine basting along the upper edge of the ruffles ⅛" on either side of the seam lines. Pull on the bobbin threads to gather.

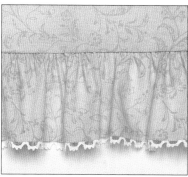

2. Attach the ruffle following steps 5 and 6 on page 85. Remove the basting thread.

ruffle with a frilled heading

Preparation

Cut a strip of fabric the desired finished depth of the ruffle, plus hem allowance on both sides. Finish both raw edges using your desired method.

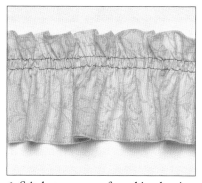

1. Stitch two rows of machine basting between the upper and lower edges. The upper allowance is usually much smaller than the one below.

2. Pull on the bobbin threads to gather the ruffle. Stitch along the center of the two gathering rows to secure the ruffle in position on the garment. Remove basting.

circular ruffle

Circular ruffles are particularly effective when made from softly draping fabrics. This type of ruffle is cut from a large circular shape with a smaller inner circle. The circumference of the inner circle is approximately the length of the edge where the ruffle is to be attached. The distance between the inner and outer edges is the finished depth of the ruffle plus hem and seam allowances. Cut the outer circle first and then cut along the straight grain through to the inner circle. Cut out the inner circle last. When the inner curved edge is straightened out and inserted into a seam, the outer curve falls into a soft ruffle.

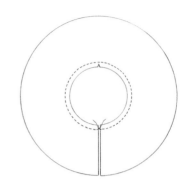

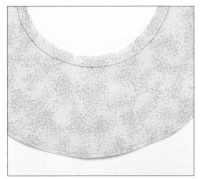 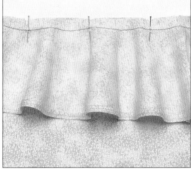 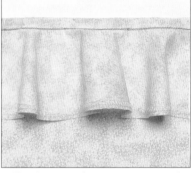

1. Stay stitch the inner circle just inside the seam line. Clip the inner seam allowances at close intervals to allow the edge to be straightened out. Finish the outer raw edge using a rolled hem.

2. Mark the center and quarters on the inner edge of the ruffle and on the edge of the garment. With right sides together and matching raw edges, pin the ruffle to the garment edge at the marked points.

3. Pin between the sections, easing the ruffle to fit the edge. Baste in place. Stitch, ensuring no pleats or puckers form in the ruffle on the seam line.

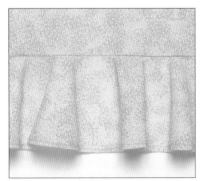

4. Trim and finish the seam. Press the seam allowances toward the garment.

hints **ruffles**

Ruffles can be an effective way to lengthen a garment.

Cut straight ruffles as a double layer when using sheer fabrics to add body and eliminate the need to hem the lower edge.

sashes

Sashes add a decorative element to the styling of a dress while controlling any excess fullness at the back. They can be constructed in various widths and from one or two layers of fabric. For a lighter finish, use a single layer which has been hemmed or finished on the sides and one end. The most common forms of sashes have straight or diagonally finished ends.

Sashes may also have shaped ends or be embellished with embroidery and lace. Embroidery and other forms of trimming are usually worked on a single layer of fabric before the sash is constructed.

Sashes are inserted into seams or darts on or near the sides of a dress. If the sash is wide, the end is gathered or pleated to reduce the width before attaching it to the garment. For each of the following methods make two sashes, ensuring they are a mirror image of each other.

single-layer sash

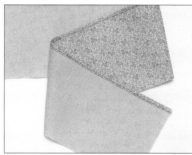

1. Cut a length of fabric the desired sash width plus seam allowances on all edges. Stitch a narrow double hem on one long raw edge.

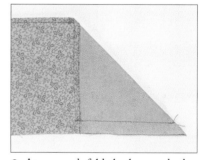

2. At one end, fold the hemmed edge diagonally to the right side, aligning the raw edges on the lower edge. Using the same seam allowance as the folded hem, stitch from the hem to the point.

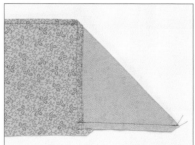

3. Trim the seam allowances to within 3/8" of the end of the stitching. Trim the point.

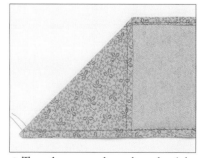

4. Turn the corner through to the right side. Fold a narrow double hem on the remaining long raw edge and stitch from the point to the opposite end of the sash. Press.

folded double-layer sash

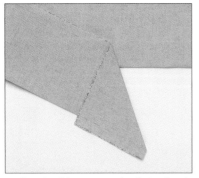

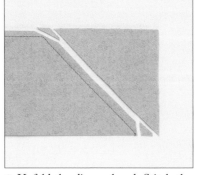

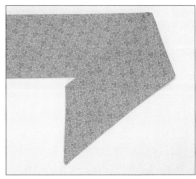

1. Cut the fabric twice the desired sash width plus seam allowances. With right sides together, press the strip in half lengthwise. Fold one end diagonally, bringing the seam line to meet the fold, and press.

2. Unfold the diagonal end. Stitch the long raw edges together and stitch diagonally across the pressed fold at the end. Trim the seam allowances and clip the corners.

3. Turn right side out. Push out the corners carefully. Press.

attaching a sash

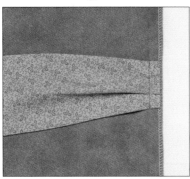

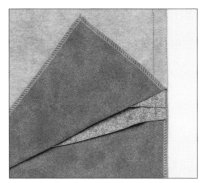

1. Fold pleats or gather the raw end of the sash to reduce the width. Baste the sash at the marked position on the garment.

2. Attach the remaining garment section, sandwiching the sash in the seam.

hints attaching a sash

At times it may be necessary to attach a sash where there is no seam to conceal the end. In that case, stitch it to the fabric with the sash lying in the opposite direction to which it will be worn. Fold the sash in the correct direction and stitch again to enclose the raw edges.

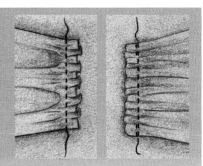

seams

A simple straight seam is the most common way to attach one piece of fabric to another. There are various other types of seams to use when the garment styling demands it. French and other self-finishing seams are ideal for sheer fabrics. Flat-fell seams provide strength as well as distinctive styling to casual clothing. Pattern instructions use a straight seam as the basis for all sewing, but will tell you when to use a different seam.

Careful preparation, accurate stitching, and precise pressing will produce a professional-looking garment. Place the pins horizontally across the seam line. This will enable you to stitch close to the pins and take them out easily as you reach them.

straight seam

In a well-formed straight seam, all the stitching is exactly the same distance from the raw edge. Generally use a plain straight stitch, set to sew 10–15 stitches per inch. One exception is a straight seam on stretch fabric, where a special stretch stitch, set to a short length, is better.

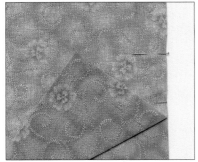

1. With right sides together and matching raw edges and markings, pin the two pieces of fabric together. Pin through the fabric perpendicularly to the seam.

2. Baste close to the seam line. As your confidence grows, basting may not be necessary; pinning will be sufficient. Stitch the seam, removing the pins just before you stitch over them.

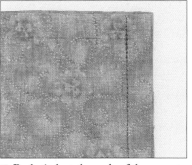

3. Backstitch at the ends of the seam to secure the stitching.

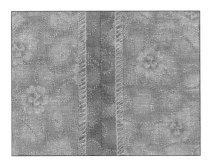

4. Remove any visible basting. Finish both sides of the seam allowances separately and press them open.

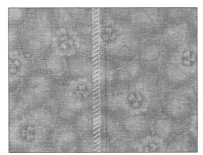

4a. Alternatively, trim the seam allowances and overcast or serge the raw edges together. Press the seam allowances to one side.

seam guide

The sole plate of your machine has a series of numbered lines or seam guides. The distance between the needle in the center position and each line corresponds with the most commonly used seam-allowance widths.

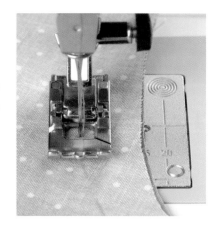

Feed the fabric under the presser foot, aligning the edge of the fabric with the appropriate seam guide to achieve an even seam. Keep your eye on the edge of the fabric until you reach the end of the seam. Stitch slowly around a curve, carefully guiding to keep the raw edges aligned with the seam guide. Avoid stopping to lift the presser foot and moving the fabric before proceeding, except on the tightest curves.

flat-fell seam

This is a self-finishing seam. A flat-fell seam is particularly suited to side seams where extra strength is needed such as on jeans legs. When finished with topstitching, it can be decorative as well as functional. This seam requires a ⅝" seam allowance.

1. With *wrong* sides facing and matching markings, pin the two pieces together. Stitch the seam.

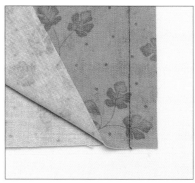

2. Trim one seam allowance only to ⁵⁄₁₆".

3. Press the seam flat. Fold the extending section of the wide seam allowance over the narrow one, enclosing the raw edge. Press.

4. Open the fabric. Press the seam allowance to the side. Pin in place.

5. Work a line of edgestitching along the fold to secure the seam.

self-faced seam

This seam works best on lightweight fabrics that don't fray easily. It requires a ⅝" seam allowance.

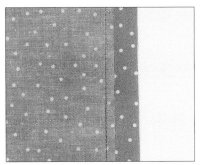

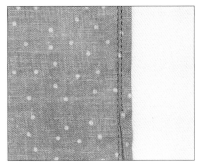

1. With *right* sides facing and matching raw edges and markings, pin the fabric pieces together. Stitch the seam. Trim one seam allowance to ³/₁₆".

2. Press the seam flat. Press under ³/₁₆" on the wide seam allowance.

3. Bring the fold to meet the previous stitching, enclosing the raw edges. Edgestitch close to the fold, sewing *only* through the seam allowances. Press the seam allowances to the right.

french seam

French seams create a beautiful finish on the inside of a garment. They are particularly suited to sheer fabrics because the seam is sewn twice, fully enclosing the raw edges. To achieve a fine French seam, start with a seam allowance of ³/₈".

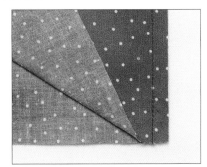

1. With *wrong* sides facing and matching markings, pin the fabric pieces together. Stitch the seam ³/₁₆" from the raw edge.

2. Trim the seam allowance to ⅛", ensuring that the edge is straight and even.

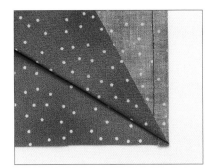

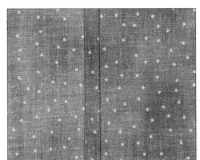

hint stitching direction

Stitch with the grain where possible to minimize stretching and puckering.

Stitch opposing seams in the same direction on both sides of the garment, such as side seams from waist to hem and shoulder seams from neck to shoulder.

3. Press the seam allowances flat and to one side. Fold the garment *right* sides together with the stitching on the fold. Press and pin. Stitch along the seam line, enclosing the raw edges.

4. Press the seam allowances flat and then to one side. Press again from the right side.

seams

125

finishing seams

To reduce bulk, seam allowances may require trimming or grading. All seam allowances with raw edges will then need to be finished to prevent fraying.

trimming

Generally, the same width seam allowance is used for all parts of a garment. Pressed open, seam allowances require little trimming. Other seam allowances will require trimming to reduce bulk and to allow a smooth line on the outside of the garment. With the seam flat, trim through both fabric layers, ensuring the edge is straight.

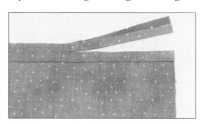

grading

After trimming, the seam may need to be graded to further reduce bulk. Trim the layers of the seam allowances to different widths, leaving the longest one to sit nearest the garment so that the seam will not cause ridges when the garment is pressed.

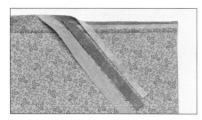

clipping corners

Points may require several clips to allow them to sit flat when turned. The sharpness of the point will determine how many cuts are required.

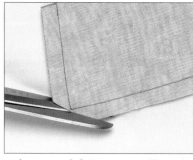

1. An outward-facing corner will require only one cut diagonally across the point.

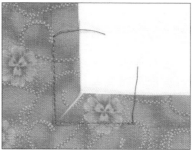

2. An inward-facing corner will require one cut diagonally into the point. Because this type of corner is stretched wide when turned to the right side, it's advisable to stitch a row of stay stitching just inside the seam allowance before clipping.

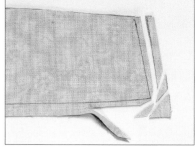

3. Trim a sharper point with at least three cuts, one diagonally across the corner as before and then two more to deepen the angle on both sides of the corner.

hints clipping

Clipping may weaken the corner of fragile fabrics. Omit the clipping and fold the corner instead. Before turning to the right side, fold and press the point.

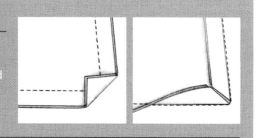

Clips into a corner should go closer to the stitching line than clipping to a seam, which is why it requires stay stitching to stabilize the corner point.

zigzag or overlock stitch

This is the quickest and easiest way to finish a raw edge. It also has the advantage of keeping the edges of the seam flat, making it less likely to cause ridges on the right side when the seam is pressed.

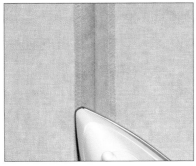

Open seam allowances. Set the machine to a suitable stitch size. Trim the seam allowances if necessary. Stitch along both edges of the seam separately. Press open.

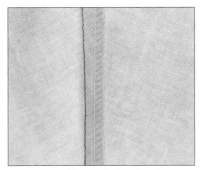

Flat seams. Alternatively, trim the seam allowances to 5/16" and finish the raw edges together. Press to one side.

turned under

This form of finishing can be used if your sewing machine doesn't have a zigzag stitch. It should only be used for lightweight fabrics. Leave the seam allowances untrimmed. Press the seam allowances open.

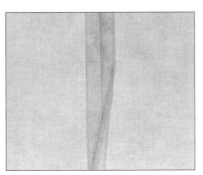

Fold under 1/8" along one raw edge and topstitch the fold. Repeat for the remaining raw edge. Press the seam again from the right side.

hint seams

The finishing method will depend partly on the fabric weight:
    Open seam allowances may show through on lightweight fabrics and should be kept narrow.
    The seam allowances on heavyweight fabrics are best finished seperately and pressed open.

bound or hong kong seam

Binding a seam makes for a neat finish and is particularly suited to heavyweight fabrics. It requires a wide seam allowance. Cut a strip of bias binding 1½" wide, or use purchased bias binding. Stitch the seam and press the seam allowances open. Bind the raw edges of the seam allowances following the instructions on page 42. Press the bound edges open. On the right side, press the seam lightly.

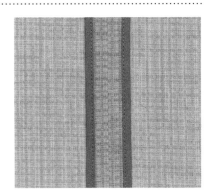

shirring

Shirring is decorative bands of gathering worked in rows across the fabric. Shirring is both decorative and practical, because it stretches to allow ease of dressing.

elastic shirring

Preparation

Wind the shirring elastic onto the bobbin by hand, stretching it slightly as you wind. Using a normal stitch length will allow the elastic to gather the fabric. Loosen the top thread tension slightly if possible. Finish the upper raw edge of the fabric if necessary.

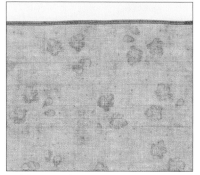

1. Mark each stitching line on the wrong side of the fabric, spaced according to the pattern. Or, mark just one line, and then use a quilting guide on the presser foot to space the successive rows of shirring.

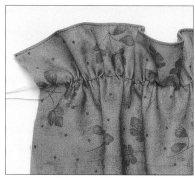

2. Leaving long thread and elastic tails at each end, stitch along the first line.

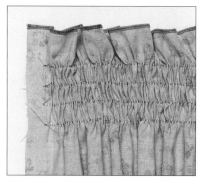

3. As you stitch each row, stretch the elastic in previous rows to flatten the fabric. Pull on the elastic tails to adjust to fit the pattern. Pull the thread tails to the back in the seam allowance and tie together with the elastic to secure.

gathered shirring

Unlike elastic shirring, this method is set in its final position, so only use it if you don't need the garment to stretch over the body. Rows of machine basting are pulled to gather the fabric. However, the rows of stitching can break with repeated wear and therefore require "staying."

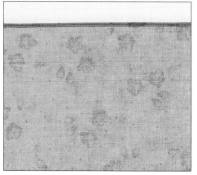

1. Prepare the fabric as described in step 1 above. Work rows of machine basting along each marked line.

2. Pull up the gathers to fit. Stitch narrow braid or stay tape behind each row to stabilize the gathers.

sleeves

Set-in sleeves are the most widely used sleeve type. They can have a smart, tailored look or appear slightly more casual depending on the method of construction or the whim of current day designers.

Another common style is the raglan sleeve. Raglan sleeves can have deep loose styling, making them suitable for coats and jackets designed to be worn over other clothing. T-shirts with close-fitting raglan sleeves can hug the body quite closely.

raglan sleeves

A raglan sleeve is attached to a garment with a seam running diagonally from the neckline to the underarm. When using woven fabrics, there is usually a dart in the middle of the shoulder to take out the fullness at the top of the sleeve. The dart shapes the sleeve to match the shoulder line. A dart usually isn't required for raglan sleeves made in knit fabric.

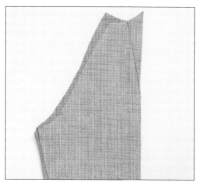

1. With right sides together and matching markings, pin and stitch the dart in the top of the sleeve, if required.

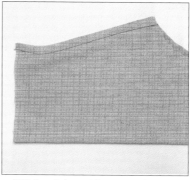

2. With right sides together and matching markings, stitch the underarm sleeve seam. Finish the seam and press the seam allowances open.

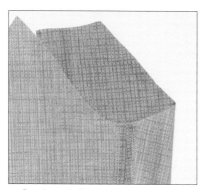

3. Stitch and finish the side seams in the bodice.

4. With right sides together and matching markings and seams, pin and stitch the sleeve into the armhole.

5. Trim and finish the seam allowances. Press them toward the sleeve.

set-in sleeves

A set-in sleeve with a smooth head, or cap, has a top curve which is slightly longer than the corresponding area of the armhole edge. Therefore the top edge of the sleeve has to be eased to fit the armhole. Generally, the goal is to achieve a smooth sleeve head without any pleats or gathers across the head, unless the sleeve was specifically designed to be gathered.

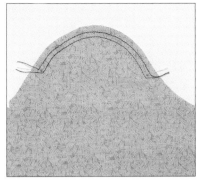

1. Stitch two rows of basting across the head of the sleeve between the marks for easing.

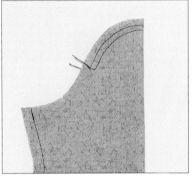

2. With right sides together, pin and stitch the underarm seam. Finish and press the seam allowances open.

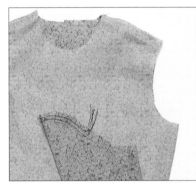

3. Turn the sleeve right side out. Leave the prepared bodice right sides together.

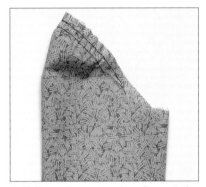

4. Pull up the easing threads until the sleeve fits the armhole. Ensure there are no gathers.

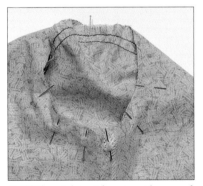

5. With right sides together and matching marks, pin the sleeve into the armhole along the lower curve between the ends of the easing. Place a pin matching the upper sleeve marking to the shoulder seam.

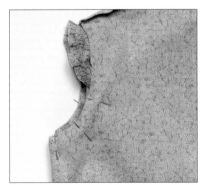

6. Pin the remainder of the sleeve to the armhole, adjusting easing as necessary.

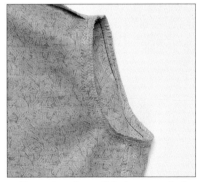

7. Baste in place. Stitch around the armhole, overlapping stitching at the underarm seam. Trim and finish the seam.

8. Carefully press the seam allowances toward the sleeve at the head using the tip of the iron. Remove any visible gathering stitches.

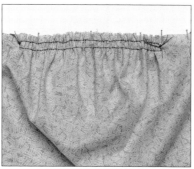

9. For a gathered sleeve head, adjust the gathering to fit the armhole as in steps 4 and 5 and secure. Finish the sleeve following steps 7 and 8.

hint set-in sleeves

For a sleeve to fit properly, the most important matching point is the shoulder seam to the mark on the sleeve head. Next, match the notch point along the front and back curves.

flat construction

Sleeves with a less-rounded cap can be attached using the flat construction method. In this method, the sleeve is sewn into the armhole before the underarm and side seams are stitched.

1. Stitch and finish the shoulder seams in the bodice.

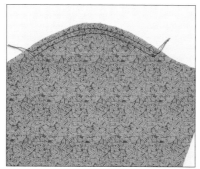

2. Stitch the rows of easing across the head of the sleeve.

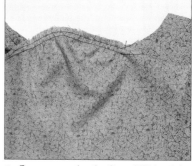

3. Open out the bodice. With right sides together and matching markings, pin the sleeve into the armhole. Adjust the stitching to ease to fit the armhole.

4. Trim and finish the seam.

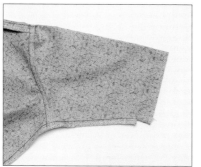

5. Matching sleeve seams, pin and stitch the underarm and side seams in a continuous line. Trim and finish the seam.

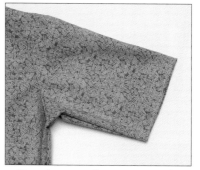

6. Press the seam allowances toward the back. Finish the lower edge of the sleeve.

sleeve finishes

A basic folded hem is the simplest method of finishing the lower edge of a sleeve. A facing, cut on the straight grain or the bias, is also a simple hemming method. This produces a firmer edge because the facing is turned under on a seam.

As well as being functional, more intricate sleeve finishes such as ruffles, bands, cuffs, casings, or bindings are usually a design feature of the garment. Often their function is to control the fullness of the sleeve at the lower edge. A ruffle or a wide binding can also be used to lengthen a sleeve if it has been cut too short or after a child's growth spurt.

It is important to determine the correct length of a sleeve before finishing the lower edge. Refer to the instructions for lengthening and shortening patterns on page 21.

one-piece sleeveband

Preparation

Apply interfacing to the wrong side of one half of the sleeveband. With wrong sides together, press the band in half. Unfold. Press under the seam allowance on the long raw edge of the uninterfaced half, and then trim the allowances to ¼". Work gathering rows on the sleeve if required.

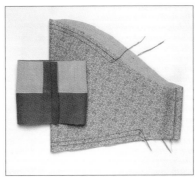

1. Stitch and finish the underarm sleeve seam. With right sides together, join the ends of the band to form a circle. Trim the seam allowances and press them open.

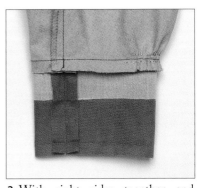

2. With right sides together and matching seams, pin and stitch the interfaced edge of the band to the lower edge of the sleeve. Trim the seam allowances to ¼". Press the band away from the sleeve.

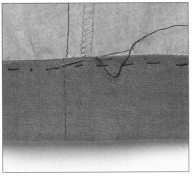

3. Matching seams, refold the band to the inside, aligning the folded edge with the previous stitching line. Pin, baste, and hand stitch in place.

4. Press carefully from the right side using the tip of the iron.

hint sleeve length

For a short puff sleeve, ensure the gathers begin and finish at the marked points on the sleeve head and lower edge. This will prevent the sleeve from twisting out of shape.

two-piece sleeveband

1. Apply interfacing to one sleeveband. Press under the seam allowance on the long raw edge of the remaining sleeveband. Trim seam allowance to ¼".

2. With right sides together, join the ends of the sleevebands to form circles. Trim the seam allowances and press open. Unfold the pressed edge.

3. With right sides together and matching seams, pin and stitch the band to the facing. Trim the seam allowances and press the facing and seam allowances away from the band. Attach the band following steps 2–4 of the one-pieced band, opposite.

piped sleevebands

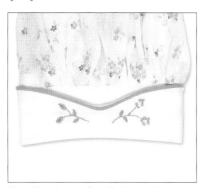

Piped and turned cuff with embroidery.

Two-pieced band with top and bottom piped edges.

Two-pieced band with piping and ruffled lace edging.

hint sleevebands

A folded hem on the lower edge of a sleeve is the only method that can be easily adjusted after it is complete. If a more complex sleeve finish has already been constructed at the lower edge and it becomes necessary to alter the length, take the sleeve out of the armhole and make the necessary adjustments to the sleeve head.

elastic casing

Preparation

Stitch and finish the underarm sleeve seam. Cut a length of fabric on the bias to fit around the lower edge of the sleeve, adding ¾" at the ends. The width should be ¼" wider than the elastic plus ½" for seam allowances on the raw edges. Press ¼" to the wrong side on both long raw edges. Unfold.

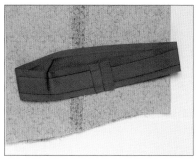

1. Using a ⅜" seam allowance and with right sides facing, stitch the ends of the casing together to form a circle. Press the seam allowances open.

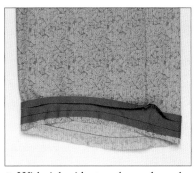

2. With right sides together and matching seams, pin the casing fold line to the sleeve seam line. Stitch along the casing fold line. Trim the seam allowances to ¼".

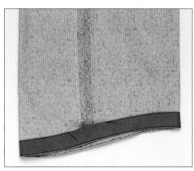

3. Rolling the seam to the edge, press the casing to the wrong side of the sleeve. Topstitch close to the edge. Leaving an opening at the underarm seam, pin and stitch the upper edge of the casing close to the fold.

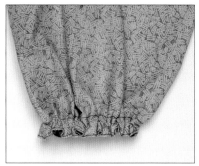

4. Insert the elastic and finish the casing following the instructions on page 57.

---

elastic casing with self ruffle

Cut and prepare the bias casing strip following the instructions above, or use purchased bias binding.

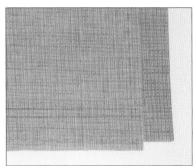

1. Mark a line across the lower edge of the sleeve at the position for the casing. Mark another line half the finished width of the casing above the first line.

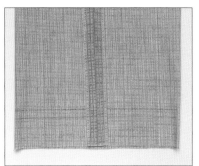

2. With right sides together, stitch the underarm seam of the sleeve. Finish both sides of the seam separately and press the seam allowances open.

3. Finish the lower edge of the sleeve. Attach the casing, insert the elastic, and finish the casing following the instructions on page 57.

faced hem

Preparation

Stitch, finish, and press the underarm seam.

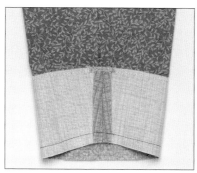

1. Cut a 2"-wide facing, following the contour of the sleeve edge. Apply interfacing to the wrong side of the facing. With right sides together, stitch the facing seam. Press open and trim the seam allowances.

2. With right sides together and matching seams, pin and stitch the facing to the lower edge of the sleeve. Trim the seam allowances to ¼".

3. Press the facing and seam allowances away from the sleeve and understitch the seam. Press the facing to the inside of the sleeve. Hand stitch the facing in place.

folded hem

1. Mark the finished length of the sleeve with pins. Finish the raw edge and press the hem to the wrong side. Unfold. Clip both sides of the seam at the fold.

2. Refold the hem and pin. Baste in place and hand stitch to secure. Alternatively, machine stitch the hem with a single line of topstitching or twin needle stitching.

hints sleeves

Check sleeve and armhole for fit and adjust the pattern pieces if required.

Take care to transfer any pattern markings to the sleeve and the armhole edge of the garment pieces.

Use appropriate pressing techniques during construction.

lapped sleeveband or cuff

This tailored sleeveband is usually found on long sleeves to allow the sleeve to open at the wrist, but can also be used on three-quarter length sleeves or short sleeves. The positioning of the button and buttonhole is important to close the band at the correct size.

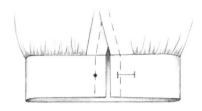

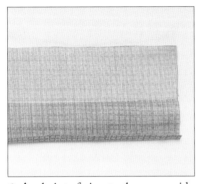

1. Apply interfacing to the wrong side of one half of the band. Press the band in half, wrong sides together. Unfold. Press under the seam allowance on the long raw edge of the uninterfaced half. Trim the folded edge to ¼".

2. Construct a lapped placket at the marked position following the instructions on page 108. Stitch the underarm seam, finish, and press it. Prepare the lower edge of the sleeve following the pattern instructions.

3. With right sides together and matching markings, pin the upper edge of the band to the sleeve with the seam allowance of the band extending past the opening of the sleeve. Adjust the sleeve to fit. Stitch, securing the ends.

4. Trim the seam allowances to ¼" and press toward the band. Fold the band right sides together, matching the folded edge to the seam. Stitch across the end even with the placket edge.

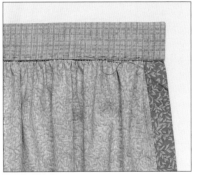

5. Turn the band to the right side, aligning the folded edge with the previous stitching line. Baste in place and hand stitch.

6. Press carefully from the right side.

topstitching

Topstitching describes one or more rows of machine stitching worked on the right side of a garment to define a seam or folded edge. While the stitching is usually decorative, it also has a practical function—securing and strengthening a seam line, or preventing a facing or lining from rolling to the right side and becoming visible.

Pleats can be topstitched to make the folds permanent or to strengthen the seamed section. Flat-fell seams are topstitched to secure and reinforce them.

Topstitching is worked at an even distance from the fold or seam, using a longer-than-normal stitch length and sometimes stronger topstitching thread. The thread color can be matching or contrasting, depending on the desired effect. It can be a single or double line of stitching. Triple lines of topstitching are sometimes featured on the side seams of jeans.

If the topstitching distance is the same as any of the seam guides on the machine, use these to position the stitching. Otherwise, place a line of tape on the machine bed to serve as a guide.

The following instructions use the distance between the needle and the edge of the presser foot to place a row of topstitching ¼" from the edge of the fabric. To adjust the width, adjust the position of the needle.

To prevent the layers of fabric from moving, it may be helpful to place a line of basting a short distance from where the topstitching will be placed.

1. Position the garment edge under the needle at the desired position. Lower the presser foot.

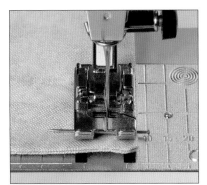

2. Stitch an even distance from the edge. As you near a corner, place a pin in the fabric the same distance from the following edge. Stitch to within one stitch of the pin.

3. Remove the pin. Turn the flywheel by hand to work the last stitch. Lift the presser foot and pivot with the needle in the fabric, realigning the next edge. Continue stitching.

edgestitching

As the name suggests, this is a row of stitching placed close to an edge. Prepare and press the seam. If necessary, baste a short distance away from the position of the stitching. Stitch through all layers, close to the edge. Remove basting.

hint edgestitching

It may be difficult to keep the stitching straight because the presser foot is suspended above the stitch plate on one side. A special edgestitching foot, which is higher on one side, can help to alleviate the problem.

understitching

Understitching is a line of stitching worked close to a seam to prevent a facing or lining from rolling to the front. Once the seam is stitched, trimmed, graded, and clipped, it is pressed toward the fabric layer where the understitching is to be placed—typically a facing. Stitch through all layers, 1/8" from the seam. If you are understitching a curve, keep the fabric flat in front of the presser foot so that you can feed it through without puckering.

decorative topstitching

Combined edgestitching and topstitching

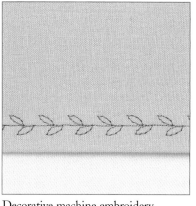

Decorative machine embroidery stitches

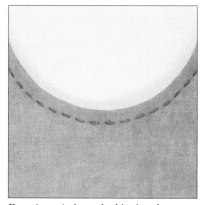

Running stitch worked by hand

tubing

Tubing is a thin strip of fabric that is seamed along the length and pulled to the right side using a tool such as a loop turner. It is often made from the same fabric as a garment and used in place of purchased cord. When the fabric is cut on the bias, the tubing is very pliable and can be shaped to follow the contours of a garment or to form loops. When tubing is to be used as a tie or straps, where it could be stretched or pulled tight, it is best made with fabric cut on the straight of grain or the stitching might break.

flat tubing

Preparation

Cut a length of fabric on the bias, twice the desired finished width plus ½" for the seam allowances. Matching raw edges, fold the strip right sides together lengthwise. Using a short straight stitch, stitch the entire length.

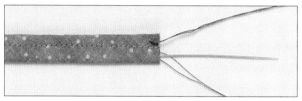

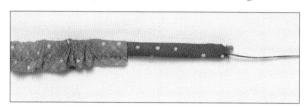

1. Trim the seam allowances. Thread a large needle with a length of strong thread and double it. Ideally, the thread should be longer than the tube. Stitch the thread securely to the seam at one end of the tube.

2. Drop the needle, eye end first, through the tube. Hold the tube vertically until the needle emerges at the opposite end. Pull gently, easing the tube through to turn it right side out.

corded tubing

Preparation

Cut a length of bias wide enough to wrap around the cord, adding a ⅜" seam allowance on both long edges. Cut the cord at least twice as long as the fabric strip.

1. Wrap the fabric around the cord with right sides together and matching raw edges. The fabric should cover half of the length of the cord. Using a zipper foot and a small straight stitch, stitch as close as possible to the cord. Trim the seam allowances to ⅛". Hand stitch the cord to the fabric at the center point of the cord to secure.

2. Easing the fabric backward from secured point, pull the enclosed cord through the tubing to cover the free end of the cord. Trim the excess cord.

tucks

A tuck is a stitched fold in fabric, used to control fullness. The width of a tuck is the measurement between the fold and the stitching. This can vary, along with the spacing between the tucks, according to the styling of a garment. Tucks hold their shape without twisting or puckering when formed and stitched on the straight grain.

Tucks are named according to the method of stitching or the spacing between them. The fold of a blind tuck meets or just covers the stitching line of the tuck beside it. Pintucks are so named because the width between the fold and the stitching line is very narrow like that of a pin. Twin-needle pintucks are a simplified method of stitching these tiny tucks by using a special machine needle with two needle shafts on a single shank.

marking tucks

Tuck positions are usually marked on a pattern piece, or sometimes a tucking guide is given so that the tucks can be stitched on a panel of fabric before the final shape is cut out. Use the pattern piece or tucking guide to mark the upper and lower positions of the tuck fold lines and then remove. Rule a line between the marks beginning at the top edge and following a thread in the fabric to the lower mark using an appropriate fabric marker.

A vertical line marking the first tuck fold line and a horizontal line marking the depth of the tucks will be sufficient if you are using a spacing guide. Alternatively all the stitching lines can be marked or the tuck width gauged as you stitch by using one of the following methods.

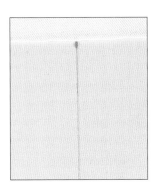

stitching tucks
gauging the width

1. Align the fold line with one of the seam-allowance marks on the machine's base plate, if there is a mark that matches the desired width of the tuck.

2. Place a piece of tape on the base plate beside the presser foot at the width of the tuck.

gauging the spacing betwen tucks

1. Use a spacing guide (a metal bar that fits into the back of the presser foot) with the bar adjusted to the width between the tucks.

2. For twin-needle pintucks, use the ridges beneath the presser foot as a guide for spacing.

basic tucks

For tucks covering the full length of a pattern piece, the stitching can be secured inside the seam allowance at both ends. Leave the thread tails unsecured if the tuck finishes before the edge.

With wrong sides together, fold the fabric on the fold line and press the fold. Stitch the tuck. Press the tuck flat and then to one side. Stitch all the tucks in the same manner, working each tuck in the opposite direction to the previous, to prevent the fabric from distorting.

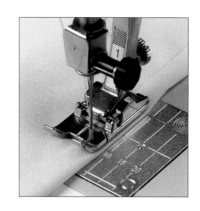

crossed tucks

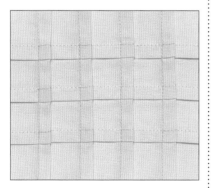

Mark and stitch all vertical tucks and press in one direction. Rotate the fabric, keeping the first set of tucks facing downward. Stitch the crossing tucks.

It is important to alternate the direction of the stitching for each tuck to prevent the panel from becoming distorted. Press the crosswise tucks carefully to one side with the tip of the iron.

pintucks

1. Fold the fabric on the marked line. Edgestitch close to the fold.

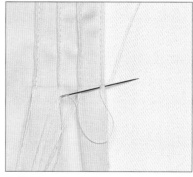

2. Fold and stitch remaining tucks. Take the top and bobbin threads separately to the wrong side at the end of the stitching.

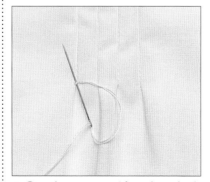

3. On the wrong side, place both threads in the needle and take several tiny backstitches through the fabric, ensuring the stitching doesn't show on the right side.

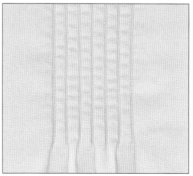

4. On the right side, press the tucks in the same direction.

twin-needle pintucks

Preparation

These delicate pintucks work best on lightweight fabrics. Mark the positions for the stitching following the previous instructions. In the following steps, the tucks are spaced using the ridges under the presser foot as a guide.

1. Holding the threads at the beginning to engage the bobbin, stitch along the first marked line.

2. Stitch the next tuck, aligning the first tuck in a groove in the presser foot. Alternatively, follow a marked line.

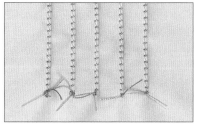

3. Take each thread tail separately to the wrong side at the end of the tuck. Tie the top and bobbin threads together snugly against the fabric. Trim, leaving short tails.

crossed pintucks

1. Mark the center tuck in both directions using an appropriate fabric marker. Stitch the first vertical tuck on the marked line. Using a spacer bar, stitch all vertical tucks.

2. Beginning with the center line, stitch the horizontal tucks in the same manner to complete the grid.

turning a corner

1. Stitch to the corner and stop with the needles in the fabric. Lift the presser foot and carefully rotate the fabric 45°. Lower the presser foot again.

2. Work one stitch, turning the flywheel by hand. Stop with the needles in the fabric. Rotate as before, aligning the foot in the next direction.

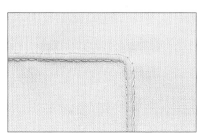

3. Lower the presser foot and continue sewing in the new direction.

corded pintucks

This type of tuck is only suitable for areas where both ends can be secured in a seam to hold the cord in place.

Preparation

Use preshrunk size 8 pearl cotton in a color to match the fabric or a darker shade for a shadow effect. Use a cording presser foot on the machine.

Secure the end of the cord on the wrong side at the start of the tuck line. Position the fabric under the presser foot, holding the cord straight. Lower the needles with the cord centered between them. Stitch along the cord.

hints **tucking**

Baste along the fold line if you are unsure about the fabric marker leaving permanent marks.

A measuring template is often helpful if there are a number of tucks to mark.

Wherever possible, press each tuck as soon as it is stitched. Press it flat first, and then in the direction it is intended to lie. This will ensure the fabric grain isn't distorted before you stitch the next tuck. Lift the tuck again and keep it out of the way when stitching the next tuck

waistbands

Most waistbands are firm, structured finishes intended to secure the waistline of a garment at the correct position on the body.

There are two main types of waistband for skirts and trousers—straight or contoured. Straight waistbands are usually the same length as the circumference of the waist plus a little extra for ease of wearing. Generally they are no wider than 2" when finished. Contoured waistbands follow the curves of the body between the waistline and the ribcage or the waistline and the hips.

For each of the following methods, construct the garment, including the zipper closure, pockets, darts, and lining if required before attaching the waistband. The upper edge of the garment may be slightly bigger than the matching distance between the markings on the waistband and will require easing to fit. Work a row of stay stitching along the upper edge of the garment.

straight waistband

Preparation

Cut out the waistband and interfacing. A straight waistband should be marked at the center front, center back, and side seams. Transfer the markings to the interfacing and apply it to the wrong side of the waistband.

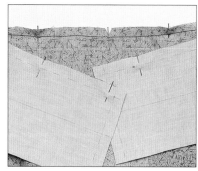

1. With the seam allowance extending at the front or back opening edges and matching marks, pin the waistband to the upper edge of the garment at the ends, centers, and seams.

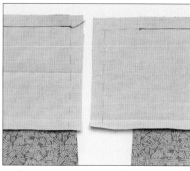

2. Continue pinning between the marks, easing the uper edge of the garment to fit the waistband. Baste and stitch in place.

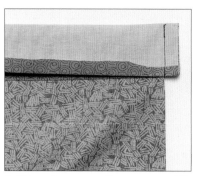

3. Trim the seam allowances to ¼". Press under the seam allowance on the remaining long edge and trim it to ¼". Fold the band right sides together at the overlapped end. Stitch across the end.

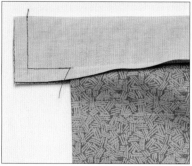

4. At the underlapped end, place the band right sides together with the seam allowances unfolded. Beginning at the opening and pivoting at the corner, stitch around the end of the waistband.

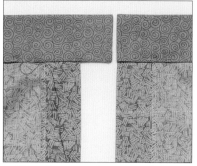

5. Trim the seam allowance and clip the corners. Turn the ends to the right side, pushing out the corners. Matching markings, pin the folded edge of the waistband to the stitching line. Hand stitch to secure. Press.

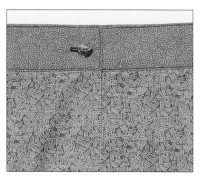

6. Work the buttonhole and attach the button to correspond. Or, attach a hook and bar for a concealed closure.

contoured waistband

Preparation

The method of attaching this is similar to a straight waistband. Apply interfacing to the wrong side of the facing pieces. Transfer markings to the interfacing. Stitch the front and back pieces together at the side seams and press open.

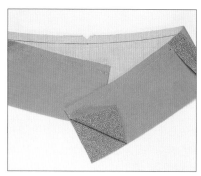

With right sides together and matching centers and seams, pin and stitch the facing to the waistband along the upper edge. Attach the waistband as for "straight waistband," above.

faced waistline

An alternative to a waistband is a faced waistline. A facing is the easiest method to finish an edge that requires shaping. The facings are generally curved to fit the finished hip and waistline curves.

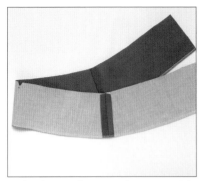

1. Apply interfacing to the wrong side of the facing pieces. With right sides together, stitch the side seams. Trim and press open. Finish the lower edge.

2. With the seam allowance extending at both ends and matching markings, pin the facing to the upper edge of the garment at the ends, centers, and seams.

3. Continue pinning between the marks, easing the upper edge of the garment to fit the waistband. Baste and stitch in place.

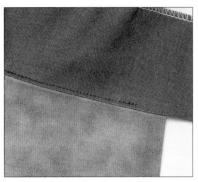

4. Trim the seam allowances and clip the curves. Press the facing and seam allowances away from the garment. Understitch close to the seam on the facing.

5. Fold under the extending ends of the facing at a slight angle. Fold the facing to the wrong side. Hand stitch the facing to the side seams and darts and along the opening edge.

zippers

Zippers are an efficient and secure way to close an opening. They can be almost invisible when inserted into a seam; or you could attach them using an exposed method to create a sporty look.

Zippers may be centered under the opening, offset to one side, or set into the seam from the wrong side using a special presser foot. Choose a zipper suitable for the style of the opening and the weight of the fabric. If you are unable to find a zipper to match the color of the garment, choose one that's a shade darker to ensure it will remain inconspicuous.

inserting a centered zipper

Positioning the top end of the zipper depends on the final finish of the opening. If a facing is to be used, such as a neckline, place the upper stop 3⁄8" below the neckline seam. If the end is to be placed under a waistband, the upper stop should be close to the seam line. Attach the zipper foot on the machine.

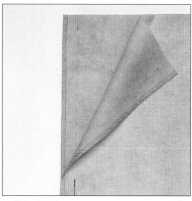

1. Stitch the garment seam to the marked point for the end of the zipper; backstitch. Finish both sides of the seam separately.

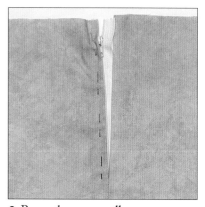

2. Press the seam allowances open, including the opening for the zipper. Pin the zipper in position, centered under the opening. Splay the top ends of the zipper tape open slightly, keeping fabric folds aligned.

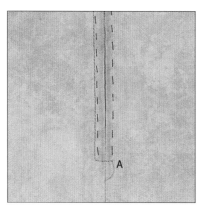

3. Baste close to the stitching line. Starting at A and pivoting at the corner, stitch across the lower end and along one side, stitching 1⁄4" from the opening.

4. Return to the lower end and stitch the remaining side in the same manner. Remove basting. Press from the wrong side on a well-padded board.

inserting a lapped zipper

Use this method when the zipper is placed at the side of a garment. To conceal the opening from the front, the lapped section is placed on the leading, or front, edge. The placement of the top end of the zipper is the same as the centered method. The instructions show a zipper set into the left side seam.

Preparation

Stitch, finish, and press the seam allowances open following step 1 of the centered zipper, opposite.

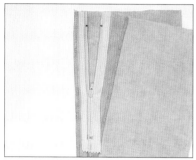

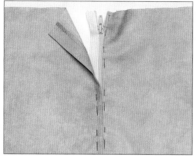

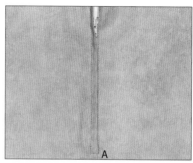

1. With right sides together and the zipper closed, pin the right-hand side of the zipper to the corresponding side of the opening. Stitch in place.

2. Turn the garment to the right side. Pin the fold close to the zipper teeth. Pin the remaining side of the zipper in place, with the lap slightly covering the fold on the right-hand side.

3. Baste in place. Starting at A, topstitch across the base, pivot, and stitch along the opening ³⁄₈" from the fold. Cut threads, start again at A, and edgestitch the remaining side to the top.

inserting a separating zipper

This type of zipper is used mostly in the front opening of casual jackets.

Preparation

Finish the lower edge of the opening. Finish the upper edge if required. Finish the raw edges of the opening. Mark the stitching lines with a fabric marker or by pressing a fold line. Place the zipper foot on the machine. Separate the zipper.

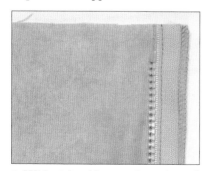

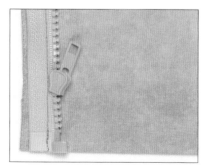

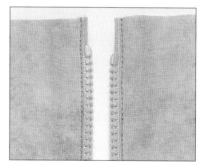

1. With right sides together, pin and stitch the left-hand side of the zipper onto the corresponding opening, aligning the stitching line close to the teeth.

2. On the right-hand side, stitch from the lower end with the slider at the top. Halfway along, stop with the needle just in the fabric. Lift the presser foot. Move the slider past the needle. Lower the foot and complete the stitching.

3. Fold both sides of the opening with the teeth on the edge. Stitch close to the fold on the right side. Work another row of stitching ³⁄₁₆" away from the first row if desired for added strength.

constructing a fly front

The following technique is used to insert a zipper in the center front of a pair of trousers. An extension, or shield, is formed behind the zipper to prevent undergarments from getting caught in the zipper teeth as the slider is moved up or down. The method of overlap has traditionally followed the same rules as a button closure—right over left for women and left over right for men—but the accepted generic position for both is now left over right.

Preparation

Apply interfacing to the fly facing and one fly shield piece.

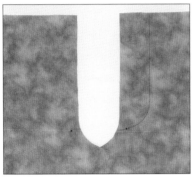

1. Mark the ends of the crotch seam and the topstitching line on the right-hand piece.

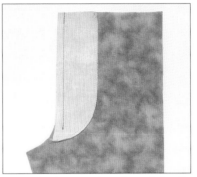

2. Finish the straight edge of the fly facing. Pin and stitch the facing to the right-hand side of the opening.

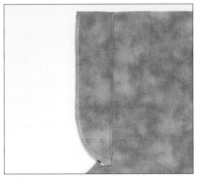

3. Trim the seam allowances and turn to the right side. Fold the facing and seam allowances away from the garment. Understitch to the top of the crotch seam.

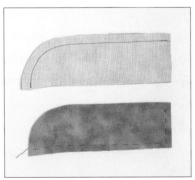

4. With right sides together, stitch the curved edge of the shield pieces. Trim the seam allowances and notch the curve. Turn right side out and press. Baste the raw edges together.

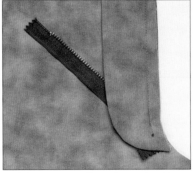

5. Aligning seam lines, baste the zipper to the right-hand opening. Matching raw edges, pin and stitch the fly shield over the zipper. Trim and finish the seam.

6. With right sides together, matching marks, and keeping the facing and shield out of the way, stitch the crotch seam. Stitch again to reinforce it.

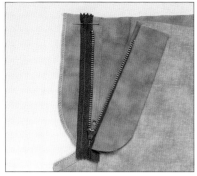

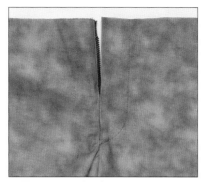

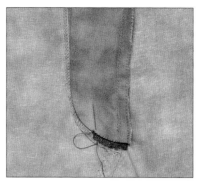

7. Pin and baste the remaining side of the zipper to the facing, placing the teeth ³/₁₆" from the seam. Stitch along the center of the zipper tape.

8. Reposition the facing on the wrong side. Keeping the fly shield out of the way, topstitch from the upper edge to the crotch seam.

9. On the wrong side, hand stitch the fly shield to the lower end of the zipper.

securing the upper end of a zipper

When setting a zipper into an opening with both ends closed, such as for a cushion back or the side seam in a dress, stitch the zipper tapes closed at the upper end of the zipper to take the strain off the stitching in the seam.

shortening a zipper

If you have a zipper just the right color and style but too long for the opening, you can shorten it. Measure the required length. Whipstitch over the closed zipper at the marked position by hand or machine. Cut off the excess zipper, leaving ¾" below the stitching if desired.

hints zippers

When stitching the seam, use a zipper foot to get as close as possible to the zipper stitching.

For the fly front and invisible zipper methods, where the seam below the zipper opening is stitched after the zipper is inserted, use a standard zipper foot to stitch that seam. This will enable you to place the stitching close against the end of the zipper.

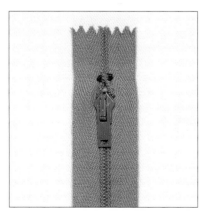

invisible zipper

This type of zipper is attached using a special presser foot. As each foot may differ slightly for different machine brands, follow the manufacturer's instructions.

The positioning of the upper end of the zipper is the same as for the centered zipper. Stitch the seam below the seam after the zipper is inserted.

Always use a zipper approximately 1¼" longer than the required opening. This is because you only can stitch to a certain point before the zipper foot is stopped by the zipper slider, causing a small amount of zipper to remain unstitched.

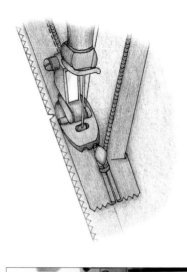

1. Finish both sides of the seam allowance separately. Mark the lower end of the zipper and the stitching lines on both sides of the opening.

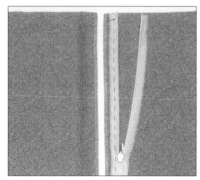

2. Open the zipper. With right sides together and aligning the coil with the stitching line, pin and tack the right-hand edge on the right-hand side of the opening.

3. Fit the zipper coil into the right-hand groove of the presser foot. Stitch from the upper edge to the lowest position possible.

4. Matching the marked ends of the seam, pin, baste, and then stitch the left-hand side of the zipper to the remaining edge of the opening. The coil sits in the left-hand groove of the foot.

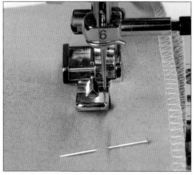

5. Close the zipper. Pin the garment pieces right sides together. Using a standard zipper foot, stitch the seam, beginning at the lower end of the zipper. Press open.

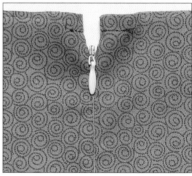

6. Shorten the zipper if required. Baste the edges of the tape to the seam allowance only.

glossary

Appliqué. Cut-out fabric shapes attached to a base layer of fabric, forming a design or pattern

Alteration. Changes made to a pattern or garment to customize the fit

Awl. Pointed-tip tool with a graduated shaft—used to pierce holes in fabric

Backing. The last or bottom layer of fabric behind others, such as in quilts

Backstitch. Hand stitch, used decoratively or to stitch seams. Reverse machine stitching used at the beginning and end of a seam to secure the stitching

Ballpoint needle. Machine needle with a slightly rounded tip—used for stitching knit fabric

Basting. Long machine straight stitch worked to temporarily join or attach—removed when permanent stitching is in place

Binding. Strips of fabric used to encase raw edges

Blind hem. Machine hemming technique using a special presser foot; a blind hem stitch

Bobbin. The spool holding the lower thread in a sewing machine

Bodice. The section of a garment worn on the upper part of the body, from shoulder to waist

Bodkin. Tool used to thread elastic through a casing

Boning. Narrow nylon or plastic strips used to create structure and shape in fitted garments

Braid. Flat decorative trim, usually containing some surface texture

Buckle. Fastening used to secure a belt or tie

Bustline. Horizontal line running around the fullest part of the bust and across the back

Bust point. Point on the pattern where the tip of the bust should sit when wearing a garment

Buttonhole. Finished opening for a button to pass through

Buttonhole stitch. Hand stitch used to finish the raw edges of a buttonhole. It resembles blanket stitch but has a looped edge.

Cap sleeve. Narrow short sleeve forming a cap over the top of the shoulder

Casing. Channel of fabric used to enclose elastic or a drawstring

Clipping. Cuts made into the seam allowance of an inward-facing curved seam

Couching. Securing cord, heavy threads, or other narrow trims to a background fabric with stitching

Covered button. Special button manufactured to be covered with fabric

Contoured. Pattern pieces cut to fit the curve of the body, enabling them to lie flat when worn

Cutting line. Outermost line of a pattern piece—the line to follow when cutting out the pieces

Dart. Tapered, stitched fold to help shape a garment to follow the contours of the body

Dress form *or dressmaker's dummy.* A dummy torso with adjustable sections used to fit a garment to particular measurements during construction

Double hem. Folding the fabric over twice to form a hem—the first fold to neaten the raw edge and the second to the depth of the finished hem

Ease. Small amount of excess fabric built into certain areas to allow for movement or to permit one edge to be shaped to fit another

Edgestitching. A row of topstitching very close to the edge of a fold or seam

Extension. Piece of fabric extending past an edge of a garment
A separate piece of paper added to enlarge or lengthen an area on a garment pattern

Facing. Piece of fabric used to finish a raw edge

Feed. The mechanical movement of fabric over the stitch plate of the sewing machine

Feed dogs. Metal teeth protruding through slots in the stitch plate—they move up and down to push the fabric under the presser foot

Finger-press. Squeezing a fold or seam between the thumb and forefinger, while rolling it or pulling it through the fingers

Finished edge. Any edge, visible or invisible, that has been stitched or serged to prevent fraying

Finished width. The actual width of any garment section after the seams are stitched, turned, and all allowances used

Fold line. Line on a pattern piece indicating a point where the garment piece will be folded

Free motion. Lowering the feed dogs to disengage the automatic feed, enabling the fabric to move in any direction

French seam. Self-finishing seam—one seam allowance encloses the other

Fusible. Material with a film of adhesive on one side that can be bonded to fabric using heat

French curve. A drafting ruler used to create curves when adapting patterns

Gathering. Method of controlling fullness when a longer fabric edge is attached to a shorter one

Grain. *Lengthwise* grain (the warp) are the threads that run lengthwise, parallel to the selvage
Crosswise grain (the weft) are the threads that run horizontally from selvage to selvage
Bias applies to any diagonal direction on the fabric. True bias runs at a 45° angle to the lengthwise and crosswise grain

Grading. Trimming back the individual layers of the seam allowance to different widths to reduce the bulk in the seam

Gusset. Square, diamond, or triangular shaped piece of fabric sewn into intersecting seam lines to provide room for movement

Heading *or flange.* Seam allowance on trim—should not be visible after the seam is complete

Hem. Fabric turned up on the edge of the garment to provide a neat finished edge

Hip. The fullest part of the hipline around the body

Hong Kong seam. Flat seam with binding used to encase the raw edges

Hook and eye. Closure that consists of the hook and a loop

Inside leg seam. Seam between the legs, running from the crotch to the hem

Interfacing. Layer of fabric or stabilizer applied to the wrong side of fabric to provide stability

Interlining *or underlining.* Layer of lining fabric tacked to the wrong side of the garment pieces and integrated into the seams during construction

Inverted pleat. Pair of mirror-image knife pleats folded toward each other. An inverted pleat folded into an opening at the lower end of the center back seam of a straight skirt is also known as a kick pleat.

Knife-edge pleat. Folded tuck in the fabric, pressed to one side

Lining. Layer of fabric used to cover or protect the inner surface of a garment; usually a separate inner layer made as a mirror image of the outer layer

Mandarin collar *also Chinese or Nehru collar.* Short standing collar extending vertically from the neckline—often with rounded corners at the front

Marking. Temporary marks made on the right or wrong side of the fabric; used to transfer the position of pattern markings

Miter. Method of neatly folding hems or flat trims so that they form a precise diagonal corner

Mockup *or muslin.* Rough copy of a garment made from cheaper fabric such as muslin, used to ensure good fit before cutting more expensive fabric. Make alterations to the muslin, take it apart, and use these pieces as the new pattern.

Nape. The upper-back part of the neck below the hairline

Needle threader. Looped wire used to pull thread through the eye of a needle

Notches. Triangular or diamond shapes appearing on the cutting lines of a pattern piece; used to match positions when garment pieces are placed together

Notching. Triangular shapes cut from outward-facing curved seams to allow the seam allowances to lie flat

Notions. Thread, buttons, zippers, and other small items used in the construction of garments

Overlocker *or serger.* Machine used for finishing the raw edges of seams—trimming and overcasting the edge and sewing, all in one action

Overlock stitch. Machine overcast stitch that encloses a raw edge to prevent fraying

Pattern. Templates needed to cut out the individual sections of a garment. Dress patterns usually contain pattern pieces printed on tissue or plain white paper and include instructions for cutting out and constructing a particular garment.

Peter Pan collar. Usually a one-piece collar with rounded ends at the center front; can also appear as two pieces with round ends at the front and back

Pile *or nap.* Describes the surface texture of short-cut fibers incorporated into the weave of the fabric, producing a soft plush surface

Pilling. Tiny balls of fiber occurring on the surface of some fabrics after repeated wear and laundering

Pintucks. Narrow tucks stitched in rows on the fabric to add decorative detail

Piping. A thin cord encased in a strip of fabric inserted into a seam

Pivot. Rotating fabric with raised presser foot and needle in fabric

Placket. Additional piece added to partial neck or sleeve opening to neaten the edges

Pleat. Precise fold or series of folds, made in the edge of the fabric to make a wider edge fit a narrower edge

Point turner. Tapered tool used to push out points and corners when turning them right side out

Pressing cloth. Cloth placed over fabric while pressing and ironing to prevent marking; can be used damp to produce steam

Pressing ham. Shaped, stuffed cushion used to support fabric while pressing curves

Princess seam. Vertical seam stitched from the armhole, over the bust, and curving into the waistline

Pucker. Rippling in the fabric on the seam line caused by incorrect pinning or stitching

Raglan sleeve. Sleeve attached to the garment from the neckline to the underarm by a diagonal seam

Raw edge. Fabric edge which has not been stitched or finished

Reinforcing. Stitching over an area again to strengthen; used in areas of most stress
    The use of interfacing to strengthen areas of stress in a garment

Reducing bulk. Trimming or grading a seam to reduce the thickness of a seam

Right side. The side of fabric that will appear on the outside; side on which the design is printed

Rolled collar. Collar that softly rolls and falls away from the neck

Rolled hem. Very narrow hem finish

Rotary cutter. Cutting tool with a circular blade ideal for making long straight cuts in fabric

Tubing. Narrow tube of fabric used for button loops or straps

Ruffle. Decorative gathered trim

Running stitch. Easy hand stitch used to hold layers together or to form decorative stitching

Rolling a seam. Bringing a seam to the edge between two layers of fabric by rolling it backward and forward between the thumb and forefinger

Satin stitch. Close zigzag stitch that creates a smooth line of close stitching

Seam allowance. Width of fabric between the raw edge and the stitching line

Seam ripper. Cutting tool designed to rip through stitching when unpicking

Selvage. Self-finished edge on both sides of the fabric; should be removed and not used in garments

Separating zipper. Zipper that separates into two parts allowing part of the garment to open completely

Set-in sleeve. Sleeve stitched into a shaped armhole

Shank. Extension at the back of a button to raise it from the fabric

Shirring. Rows of machine gathering or narrow elastic used to gather and control fullness

Sizing. Starchy fabric finish used to stiffen limp fabric

Slash. An opening cut into the garment

Sleeve head *or cap.* Upper curved section of sleeve, between the marks indicated on the pattern piece

Slip stitch. Hemming stitch through a folded edge

Slubs. Lumps of fiber in the fabric weave, causing an uneven surface

Spool *or spindle.* The top thread holder on a sewing machine or a reel of thread

Stabilizer. Layer of fabric or interfacing applied to the wrong side of the garment piece to provide strength or stability

Stay stitching. Line of stitching done to stabilize fabric and prevent unwanted stretching prior to seaming—usually placed just inside the seam line on curved edges

Stay. Fabric or tape used to reinforce an area or to prevent stretching

Stitch in the ditch. Stitching in the folds between the seam while pulling the fabric tightly from the left and right to expose the seam

Stitching line *or seam line.* Line defining the division between seam allowance and garment; the position to place stitching

Tailor's tacks. Way of marking placement points on garments for buttonholes, darts, pockets, etc.

Tear-away. Easily torn stabilizer used as temporary firmness behind stitching

Tension. Tautness of the machine stitch. On a sewing machine there are two types of tension—thread and bobbin.

Topstitching. Decorative row of stitching parallel to a seam or edge

Tuck. Fold stitched in the fabric and pressed to one side

Trim. Thin decorative strip such as ribbon or lace
     Cutting away excess fabric from seam allowances

Turning through. Pieces stitched right sides together before turning the right side to face outward with the seam allowances enclosed within

Twin needle. Pair of needle shafts secured into a crossbar extending from a single shank

Underlap. The lower section of two overlapping pieces

Underlining. Layer of fabric behind the main piece. Provides reinforcement and support to the garment fabric

Understitching. Row of stitching through seam allowances and facings, very close to seam; used to stop lining or facings from rolling out

Universal needle. The sewing-machine needle suited to most sewing tasks

Vent. Lined opening allowing for movement when garment is worn

Waistband stabilizer. Heavyweight woven band with a line of reinforced stitching to prevent it from folding or rolling when stitched into a waistband

Walking foot. Machine presser foot used to provide even tension and feed on the upper surface of the stitching; works in unison with the feed dogs underneath

Warp *or lengthwise grain.* Term describing the yarns running along the length of woven fabric

Weft *or cross grain.* Yarns running at right angles to the lengthwise yarns of woven fabric

Welt. Separate fabric strip, often used in the finishing process of a slash pocket

Whipstitch. Hand stitch used for holding a fold in position or joining two edges together

Wrong side. Unfinished or less defined side of the fabric; inside of the garment

Yardage. The amount of fabric needed to complete a project for a specific size

Yoke. Section of garment that sits flat across the shoulder and neck area or from waist to hip

Zigzag stitch. Diagonal machine stitch produced with a side-to-side movement; used to produce a decorative finish, finish raw edges, or to join two edges butted together

Zipper. Fastener consisting of two rows of metal, plastic, or nylon teeth on strips of twill tap and a slide that draws the teeth together to close an opening

index